Waterfowl Illustrated

WATERFOWL
ILLUSTRATED

by Tricia Veasey

Schiffer Publishing Ltd

Box E, Exton, Pennsylvania 19341

To my father, William Veasey,
whose ability to conceive
is rivaled only by
his ability to manifest

Printed in the United States of America.
ISBN: 0-916838-89-7
Published by Schiffer Publishing Ltd., Box E, Exton, Pennsylvania 19341.

Introduction

In Charlotte, North Carolina, there is a place called Freedom Park. In 1982, I was invited to show there. I accepted but ultimately could not attend so in my place went my daughter Tricia. At twenty-three, she was already a published writer, a prize winning waterfowl carver, an accomplished carving teacher, a poet and at that point was just beginning to realize that her photography was an integral part of my first book, *Waterfowl Carving, Blue Ribbon Techniques.* Armed with this background, Tricia took Freedom Park by storm and has since informed me that it is now hers. I shall be content to view Freedom Park through her eyes. Her eyes "see" things that mine and probably yours do not. Those of us who realize this and allow her to "see" for us will have a distinct advantage.

In this book, Tricia "sees" the things we need to see as artists, giving us the whole as well as the several parts. I have on many occasions bought a book for one photograph I wanted, and often it was not wonderful. Tricia has painstakingly assembled the most needed and usable photographs in color and black and white of most of the North American waterfowl species. Much of her photography appears to be three-dimensional. I do not know how this occurs, I can only appreciate that it does. There is a dynamic quality which jumps out from the picture. Therefore, in addition to being a source book of the many parts of waterfowl, this book also contains a wealth of artistic beauty in individual photographs of particular live birds in spectacular natural settings.

I know Tricia's ability, I have never doubted it. It is, however, always pleasant to see a completed project. The only predictability is that the project will be well done. This leads me to the inevitable conclusion that she has attained "mastery" and that this will be exemplified in all that she does. *Waterfowl Illustrated* is destined to become one of the major source books for carvers, painters and taxidermists working in the waterfowl field.

William Veasey

Acknowledgments

I extend here a very sincere thank you to my father, William Veasey not only for affording me this opportunity, but for creating and supporting it as well. Thank you also to my publisher, Peter Schiffer for believing in me as an artist to the extent of backing this major project.

I would like to acknowledge Mike and Yetta Dison, without whose exquisite taxidermy work this book would not have been possible. Thank you as well to taxidermist Roger Everett whose beautiful work appears throughout the book.

Dr. David Niles and Gene Hess were extremely helpful at the Delaware Museum of Natural History.

Clarence Webb of Elkton, Maryland has raised many of the ducks and geese that appear live in the book. I'd like to thank him for having them and for allowing me to photograph them whenever I needed to. I also appreaciate having been able to photograph the swans owned by R.E. Lee Andrew of Easton, Maryland.

I want to thank my family, from Mom all the way to my nieces and nephews for fully supporting me through this 'ordeal' of bookmaking, and Dave Ormond just for being there.

Table of Contents

Black and White Studies and Text

opposite page Mute Swan, Wells, England

Mute Swan, note wing feather pattern

Color Studies

Swans

Mute on water, note bill detail

Young Mute head, note bill color and detail

Mute Swan, classic pose

Young Mute Swan, note mottled feathers, size of feet

Trumpeter, note kink in neck

Head close-up, note bill detail and mottled feathers in moult

posite page One-year old Trumpeter Swan

One month old Trumpeter cygnets

Trumpeter pair with cygnets, note carriage of heads

Snake neck position, feathers in moult

Elegant Trumpeter pose

Pair with cygnets

One year old male, will be fully white after this moult

Whooper Hen with cygnet

Second nest of the season for this Whooper pair with one surviving egg, this occurance is very rare

Whooper Swan

Atlantic Brant

Geese

Brant head, note small bill and white streaks

Close-up of chest, note feather pattern

Overview of tail, tertials and primaries, note white tail
coverts out nearly to end of tail in center

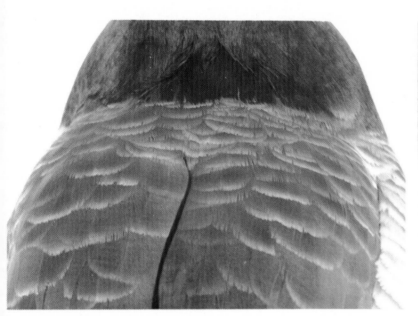

Brant back, note feather pattern

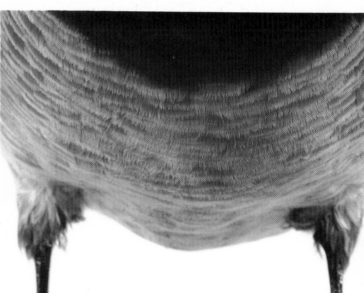

Brant belly, note not all white

Side, note feather pattern and color

Brant back, another view.

Floating Blue Goose, wings tertials drooped over the side, note how tightly the tail is held—see Snow Goose

Standing in water about to lift foot, note grayish patch of secondaries and coverts not revealed in relaxed positions

Blue Goose

Standing Blue, note foot color and shape

Blue Goose feeding

Blue Goose gander with Canada gander

Blue Goose, alert but not enough to rise

Blue Goose floating with Canada, note difference in size,
carriage of heads and of tails

Blue Goose gander standing with a Canada Goose
gander, these two pair up every year

Pair of Canada Geese on nest, most of their nests are this
large

Canada Goose, note how much chest is in water

Alert live Canada Goose, note bill detail

Canada Goose alert not yet defensive

Canada Goose closed wing and side detail

Canada Goose drinking, note bill detail

Canada Goose

Resting Canada Goose

Canada Goose chicks, note neck positions already adults

Scolding Canada Goose

Canada stretching wings, foward wing is pinioned

Canda Geese

Classic standing Canada Goose

Canada Goose, defensive position

Emperor Goose drinking

Alert, note head position

Pair at rest

Resting Emperor Goose, note head position

Sleeping Red-Breasted Goose

Red-Breasted Goose on water

Front view

Red-Breasted Goose pair

Note long primaries and short tail

Note one wing is pinioned

Snow Goose pair, one observing, one scolding

Floating Snow Goose, chest low in water, note bill color and detail

Feeding pair, note texture of neck feathers and bill and foot color

Standing Snow Goose, note primaries falling down in
relaxed position

Feeding Snow Goose

White-Fronted Goose pair feeding, note necks resemble
Canada Geese in this position

Resting White-Fronted Goose, wings dropping slightly on
the sides

Pair, note white band between the wings and the sides

White-Fronted Goose

Back of White-Fronted Goose, notice separation of feathers on neck, unlike smooth necks of the Canadas.

Feeding, note neck position

White-Fronted Goose standing in water, note staggered
tertials

Foraging in the pond edge for food

Wigeon Drake floating, note bill color and size and iridescence on head

Surface Feeding Ducks

Hen floating with drake

Pair entering water, hens chest held low

Wigeon Drake

Wigeon pair floating

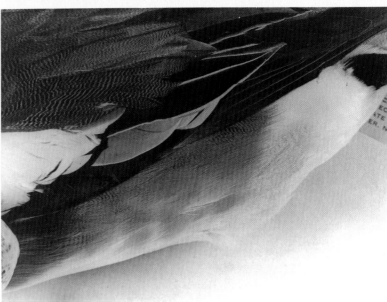

American Wigeon drake head, note iridescent green patch

Drake secondary patch, note green iridescence

Drake back and side

Drake primaries and tail, note long center tail feathers

Drake secondary, primary and tertial section

Drake tail underneath for detail

Floating Black Duck, note bill shape and color

Drake, tail up off water

Black head, disregard bill color

Open wing secondaries, notice clean lines of this duck

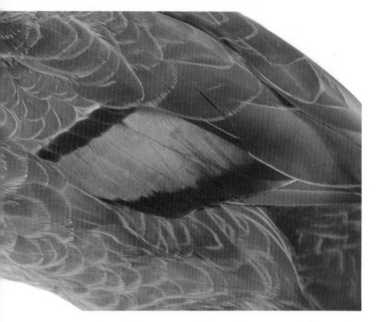

Side, note purple iridescence on secondaries

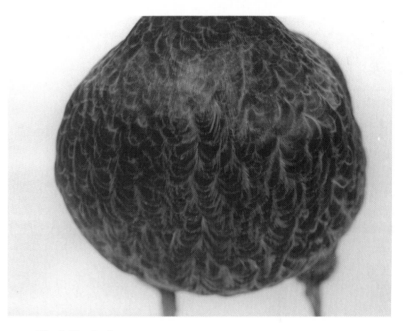

Black Duck chest

Black Duck tail detail

Standing Black Duck looks like the Mallard in shape

Blue-Winged Teal Drake swimming, note chest low in water, head extended

Pair walking, note exentuated roundness of their bodies

Drake with head slightly raised to swallow

Blue-Wing Drake feeding

Hen drinking

Blue-Wing Hen relaxed, note size and shape of bill

Drake upper wing and secondaries, note blue patch for which they are named

Hen, iridescence less prominent at this angle

Drake head, bill painted

Hen head, note pronounced lightness under neck and small light ring around eye

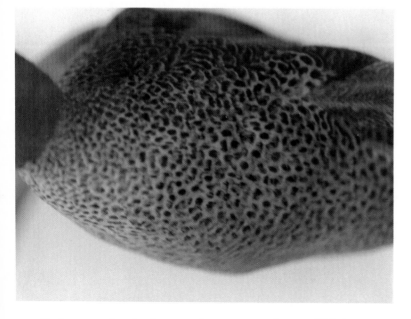

Drake, note dots begin to get larger, toward rear of bird

Hen chest

Drake walking, note length and shape of bill

air floating, drake alert

Hen floating, head alert

tanding drake, blue patch not as prominent

Floating Cinnamon Teal Drakes at height of breeding plumage

Cinnamon Teal Hen, difficult to distinguish from the Blue-Wing hen

Drake standing, note shape of bill

Pair in water, note shape of hens bill

Cinnamon Teal Drake

Hen, note feather pattern

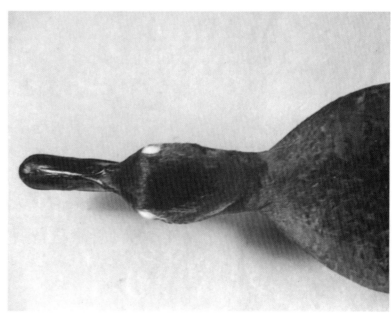

Top of Drakes head, note bill detail

Drake head, note bill shape

Drake primary and tertial area detail

45

Swimming Gadwall Drake

Pair, both with heads in alert positions

Drake mating with hen, hen submerged

Drake chest, side, note graduation of feather pattern towards back

Drake rump-side, tail small

Drake wings pulled up, not only tertials are pointed

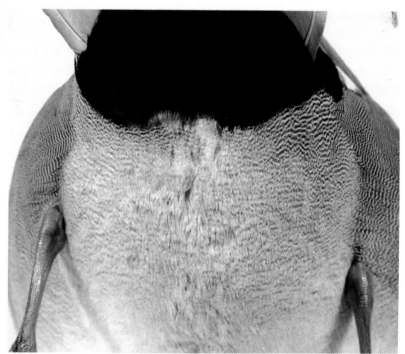

Underneath Drake

47

Drake head, notice looks like mallard hen with less brown
through eye patch, bill painted

Drake side, shoulder, note vermiculations

Green-Winged Teal pair, note head positions

Hen standing, note small bill and iridescent green patch

Drake floating with head alert, note foot placement

Underneath drake rump, note yellow patches

Drake side, note white patch which distinguishes him from the European Teal

Drake rump area, note tertial placement

Drake back and tail detail

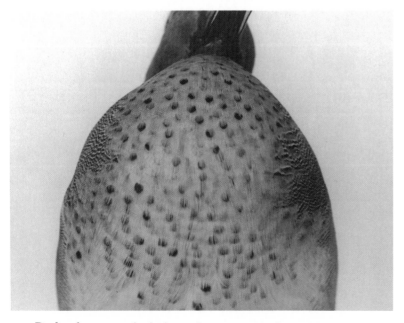

Drake chest, vermiculations often seen on edges of chest as well as the sides

Pair, floating, drake alert

Hen head detail

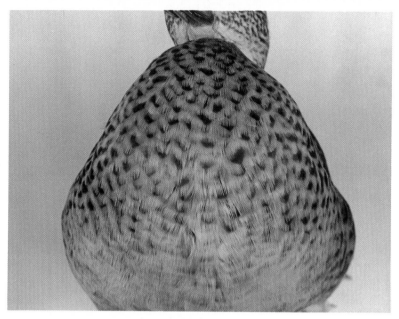
Hen chest, note feather pattern

Hen back, note feather shapes and pattern

Hen primaries, secondaries and tail, note also secondary coverts

Hen detail of back of head

Hen, underneath tail detail, note rump color

Mallard Hen, scolding

Mallard hen in Wells, England

Mallard chick on nest

Mallard pair, note proud carriage of chest in male

lert drake with hen, notice foot position

rake, note slight purplish iridescence on back of head

Handsome drake, notice nagging wife in background

53

Mallard pair, note bill and feet colors

Drinking Mallard Drake, head up to swallow

Hen standing relaxed

Floating Drake, note tail position

Hen head, bill painted

Hen rump, note color pattern on tail feathers

Feeding Mallard Hen

Roll call!

Mallard Drake head, notice iridescent sheen

Drake wing extended, secondaries iridescent blue

Drake rump area, primaries neatly crossed

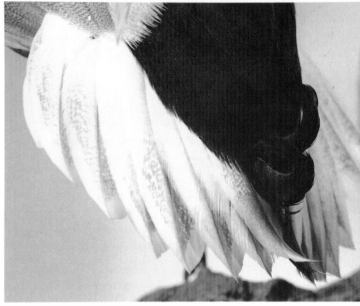
Drake tail, note heavy vermiculations in interiors of tail feathers and dark quills

Drake secondaries, side feathers laying over edge

Underneath Drake rump, feet painted

Hen rump underneath, note also color pattern

Hen wing, iridescence not showing from this angle

Light patch under hen head

Hen back, wings extended

Pintail pair, the hen is more slender than the mallard hen she resembles

opposite page   Drake standing in water, note bill color

Pintail Drake, note slight green iridescence on back of head

Drake standing, note foot color and body shape

Pair feeding on edge of pond

Hen rump area, tertials slightly rounded

Drake rump, note shape of tertials and tail coverts

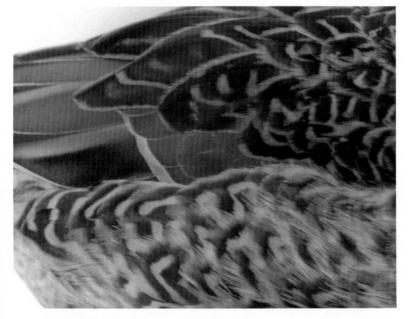

Hen side

Hen back, note shape of feathers

Drake upper back, wings spread

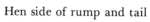
Hen side of rump and tail

Drake side, note light yellow patch on rump

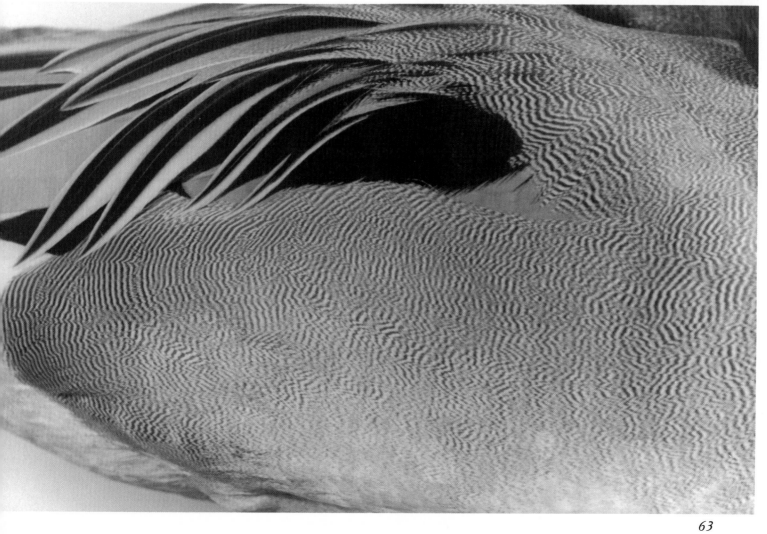

Hen head in sleeper position

Drake head preening, note white streak in this position

Extended drake wing, iridescence not visible at this angle

Under drake wing

Shoveler Drake, note green and purple iridescence on head and unusual shape of bill

Shoveler Hen preening chest, notice light blue patch above secondary coverts on wing

hoveler Hen preening wing

Preening under wing

hoveler Hen

With her one clipped wing she attempts to regain balance
fter stretching wings

Hen takes a rest from her labors

Floating Shoveler Drake, head greenish

Preening Shoveler Drake

Drake back, note purplish head

Drake swimming

Floating Wood Duck Drake

Woodie pair resting, hen in classic stance with one foot up and head resting down against chest

Drakes on water, note head down on chest and crest laying out from the head on back

Hen, bill painted

Hen chest

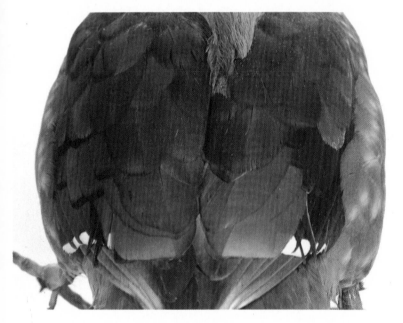

Hen back, note squareness of tertials

Hen side, note iridescence in primaries, on back and on secondaries and coverts

Rump area of hen, there is even a slight iridescence on the tail feathers

Underneath tail of hen

Drake head, note irridescent colors, bill painted

Drake back and side, note slight iridescence in patch on side of rump

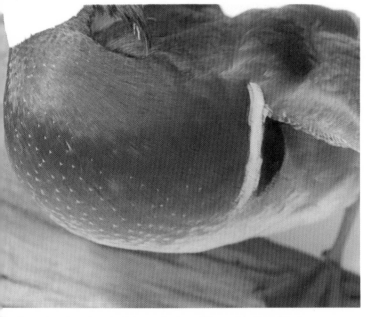

Drakes chest, color and hue changes from bird to bird

Underneath tail and wing of drake

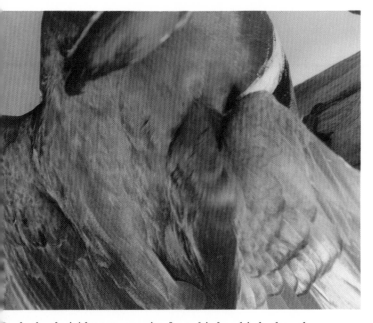

Drake back, iridescence varies from bird to bird, though all Woodies secondaries and coverts are brighter

Wood Duck Drake

American Goldeneye Drake, note size of feet

Diving Ducks

Drake, tail on water

American Goldeneye Hen swimming, note foot positions

Goldeneye pair, hen often skims along water with head nearly level with body and tail flat on water

Hen on water, head feathers ruffled

Drake relaxed, tail down, head not as puffed

Drake mating, hen submerged

Pair, drake alert and hen resting

Barrow's Hen floats low in water and skims along the surface

Alert drake, note puffiness of head

74

Hen distinguished from the American by bill color

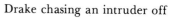
Drake chasing an intruder off

Barrow's Goldeneye Drake, note half moon white patch on face and white spots in the black on the back

Bufflehead Drake head, note all the different iridescent colors

Bufflehead hen, tail on water

Alert Drake, tail on water

air resting on water

Drake back, tail spread, feet painted

rake side, black feathers into the white

Bufflehead, back of head detail

rake head, bill painted

Drake side

Canvasback Drake, tail down on water

Canvasback Hen, note tail

Drake, note carriage of chest in water

78

Hen head, bill painted

n primary and tertial area

Drake rump area, tail quills dark

Drake wing and shoulder

Drake head, bill painted

Drake, bill and feet painted

Oldsquaw drake mount

Head detail, note the white around the eye

Tertials and back detail

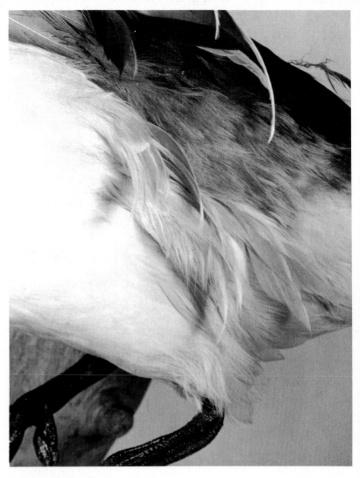

Side detail

Tail detail, note pin-feathers

Close-up of under wing detail

Scaup Drake, note tail position and bill color

Scaup Hen, bill painted

Scaup Drake, bill painted

83

Scaup Drake, note slight green iridescence on back of head

Hen head, Bill painted

Vermiculations on back of drake

Hen side, note different vermiculations in different areas

Drake rump area, rounded tertials and small primaries

Hen chest, feathers slightly ragged on ends

Red Head Drake, tail in water, note head feathers slightly ruffled.

Alert Red Head Drake, note eye color

Red Head Hen, tail up

Red Head pair, drake preening

Hen relaxed on water

Drake relaxed on water

Hen swimming, note position of head

Drake, head slightly up to swallow water

Red Head Drake feeding, note foot color

Swimming Drake, note tail position

opposite page   Redhead hen mount, notice the white up on the side

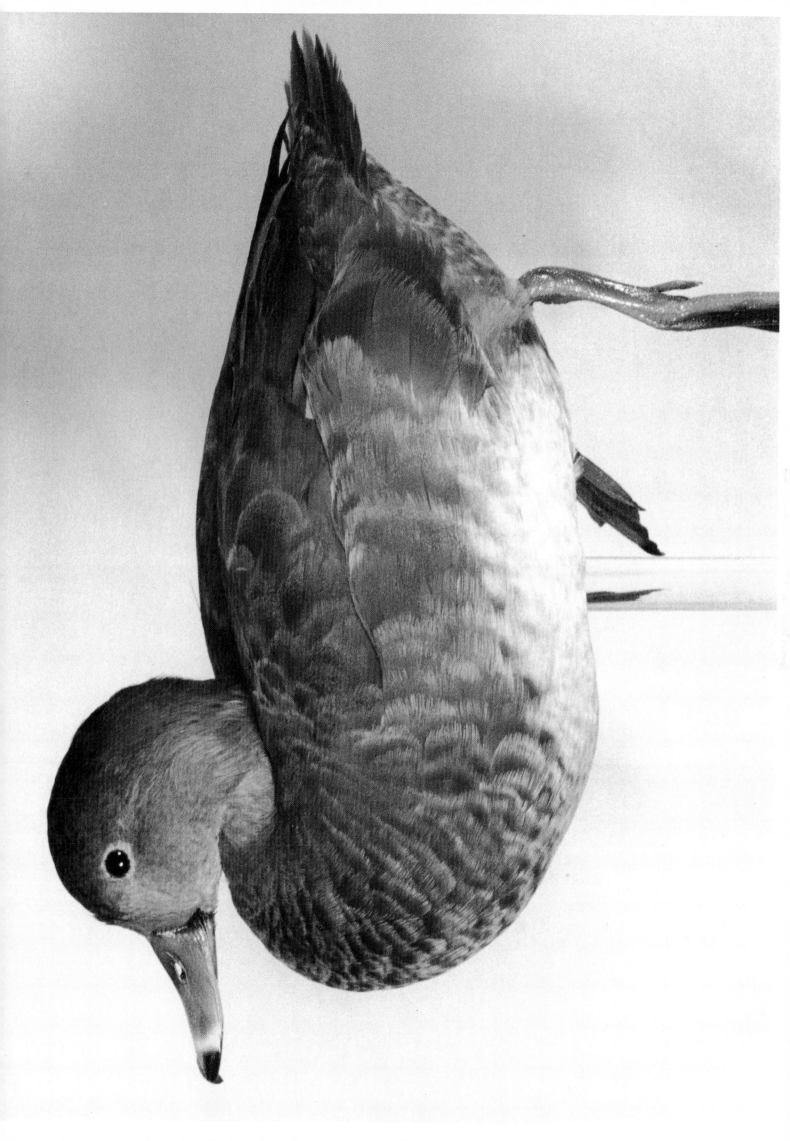

Back of hen for feather pattern

Close-up hen head, note light circle around the eye

Hen rump and side detail, note secondary patch

Hen chest and side for feather pattern

opposite page. Redhead drake mount, note small tail and large feet

Back of Redhead drake, note feather pattern

Drake head, bill painted

Rump and tail area of drake

Chest and side area, drake

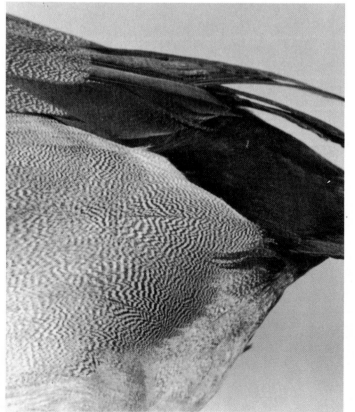

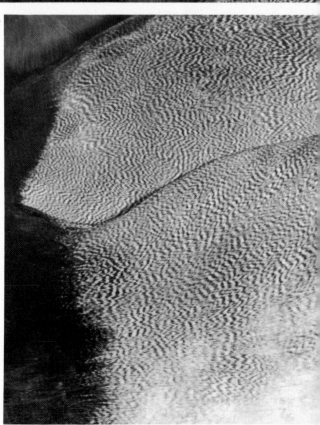

Ring-Necked pair, hen alert, drake relaxed

Drake, note size of foot and indistinct ring around neck

Hen, note tail position and bill color

Drake, note tail position

Drake, mount

Drake swimming

94

Hooded Merganser Drake, crest held fully puffed to attract hen during mating season

Mergansers

Hen wrestling with fish, note tail flat on water

Pair during mating game, drakes crest up, hens tail up also

Hooded Merganser Drake

Hen on water, crest slightly puffed

Drake head, bill painted

Hen resting with fish in bill, note position of feet

Back of drakes head

96

Red-Breasted Merganser Drake full side, bill and feet
painted

Hen head, note bill shape

Hen back and primary detail

Drake head, note thinness and position of crest feathers

Drake rump detail, note small primaries, feet painted

Drake side detail, note vermiculations only go half way down

Drake, note vermiculations on rump

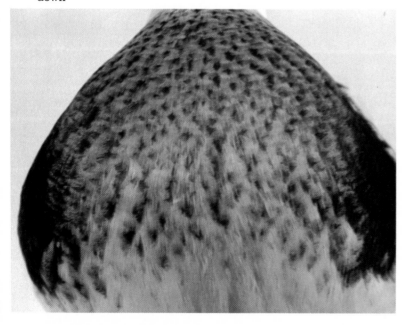

Drake chest, dots get larger towards bottom

Drake back, note large secondaries

Ruddy Duck drake, note bill color

Ruddy Duck

Ruddy Hen, tail flat on water, note foot position

Ruddy pair, note tail positions and drake 'horns'

Courting drake, note tail full up

Drake swimming, note tail

Ruddy hen, tail on water

Ruddy pair, note drakes tail not spread and 'horns' pronounced

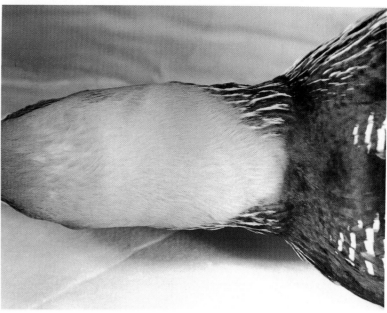

Arctic Loon head, note soft blend between white and black on face

Top of a head and neck detail, note blending on the front of crown

Loons

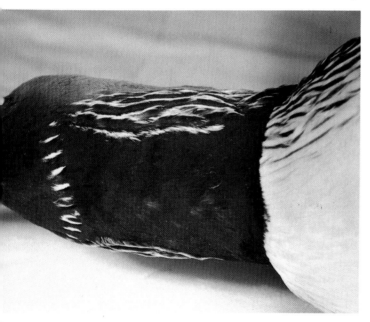

Detail underneath the head

Arctic Loon back, note pattern of white patches

Primaries and rump detail

Side, note black and white blending

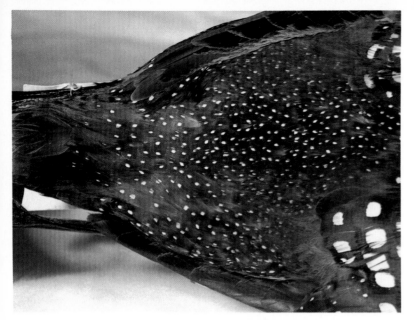

Common Loon rump and tail detail, note small tail

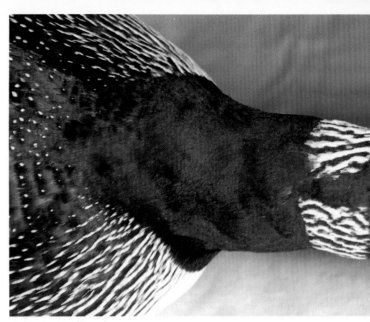

Neck of Common Loon

Back detail

Side of chest

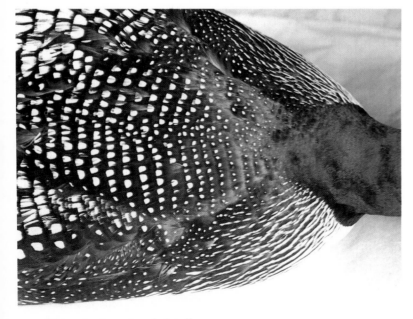

Upper back and neck detail

Side and feather detail

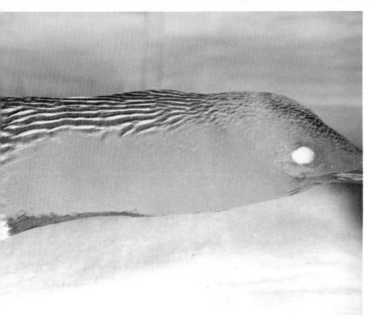
Ruby-Throated Loon head

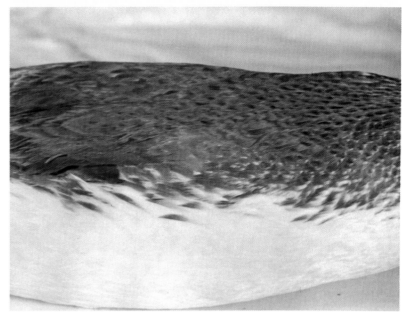
Side view for feather detail

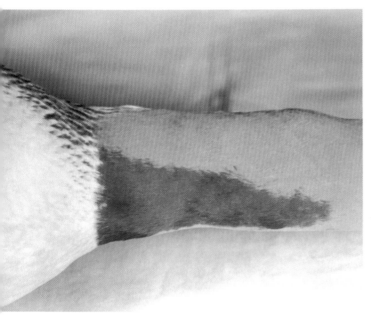
Underneath head, note 'ruby' patch

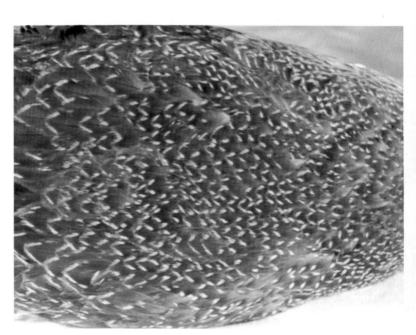
Back feather detail, pattern very unlike Yellow-Billed and Common Loons

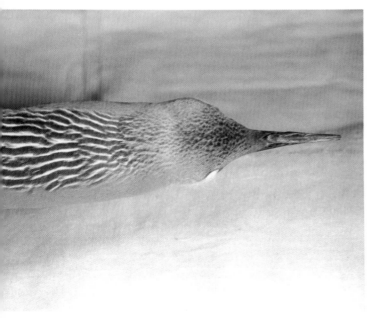
Top of head, note dots toward front turn to streaks at back

Rump area, note primaries

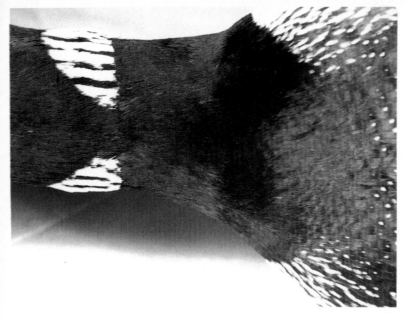

Yellow-Billed Loon neck, similar to Common Loon

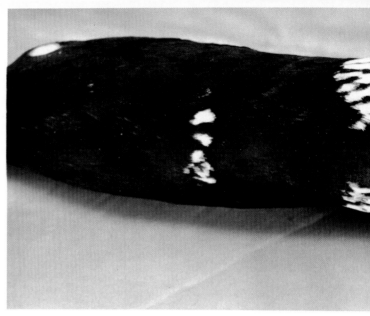

Underneath head and neck, note white pattern

Primary and tail area, note how small the tail is for this large bird

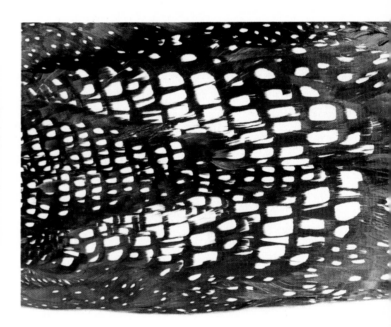

Back detail, note busy white pattern

Side and back detail

Side and upper back

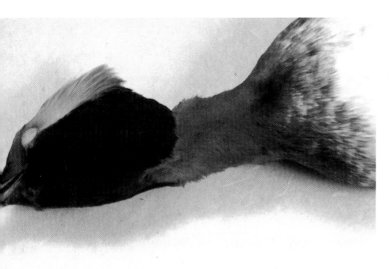

Eared Grebe, head, chest and bill detail

Head, separate angle for study

Grebes

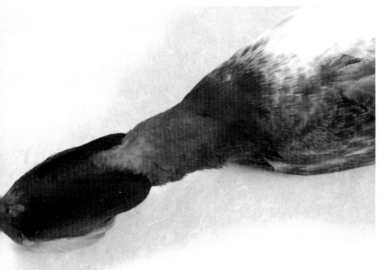

Underneath head and chest, and side detail

Back and rump area, no visible tail

Side detail, note white extends up onto the side

Upper back feathers for detail

Wildlife Refuges and Other Preserves

The best places to closely observe waterfowl are in zoos. They are ideal for photographing as they are usually designed to allow the birds only a limited distance from the spectators. The following zoos have very good collections of waterfowl: The Philadelphia Zoo, Philadelphia, Pennsylvania; The Baltimore Zoo, Baltimore, Maryland; The Salisbury Zoo, Salisbury, Maryland; The San Diego Zoo, San Diego, California.

Natural history museums are very useful for viewing mounted birds and skins. The Delaware Museum of Natural History, Wilmington, Delaware, for example, has an extensive collection of waterfowl skins containing nearly all the North American species. They also usually will allow the skins to be borrowed for special projects. Most of the mounts photographed for this book were prepared by Mike and Yetta Dison and Roger Everett. In every state, zoos and natural history museums can be very helpful. Visit them and find out what they have.

Other places to observe waterfowl are wildlife refuges and state preserves. The following list of many of the refuges and preserves in North America includes the birds one can expect to find in each.

Wildlife Refuge
Northeastern States
Delaware:

Bombay Hook National Wildlife Refuge
R.D. 1, Box 147, Smyrna, Delaware 19977
Location: 9 miles southeast of Smyrna, just off Route 9
Waterfowl: Black Ducks, Mallards, Gadwalls, Pintails, Wood Ducks, Green-Winged Teal, Blue-Winged Teal, Widgeons (*Wigeons*), Shovelers, Ring-Necked Ducks, Greater Scaup, Lesser Scaup, Buffleheads, Ruddy Ducks, Hooded Mergansers, American Mergansers, Canada Goose (*Geese*), Lesser Snow Goose (*Geese*)

Little Creek State Wildlife Area
Edward Tatnall Building, Legislative Avenue and William Penn Street, Dover, Delaware 19901
Location: Route 9, just east of Dover
Waterfowl: Black Ducks, Canada Goose (*Geese*), Gadwalls, Pintails, Shovelers, Green-Winged Teal, Blue-Winged Teal, Widgeons (*Wigeons*), Ring-Necked Ducks, Greater Scaup, Buffleheads, Ruddy Ducks, Hooded Merganser, Canada Goose (*Geese*), Lesser Snow Goose (*Geese*)

Prime Hook National Wildlife Refuge
Box 195, Milton, Delaware 19968
Locations: Approximately 22 miles southeast of Dover
Waterfowl: Varied species of ducks, Canada Goose (*Geese*), Lesser Snow Goose (*Geese*)

Maine:

Moosehorn National Wildlife Refuge
Calais, Maine 04619
Location: Northeastern States, Maine, on Route 1
Waterfowl: Canada Goose (*Geese*), Ring-Necked Ducks, Black Ducks

Petit Manan National Wildlife Refuge
Moosehorn National Wildlife Refgue
Calais, Maine 04619
Location: Northeastern States, on Route 1
Waterfowl: Green-Winged Teal, Black Ducks

Maryland:

Blackwater National Wildlife Refuge
Route 1, Box 121, Cambridge, Maryland 21613
Location: Eastern shore
Waterfowl: Varied species of ducks, Mallards, Canada Goose (*Geese*)

Eastern Neck National Wildlife Refuge
Route 2, Box 225, Rock Hall, Maryland 21661
Location: Eastern Shore, Kent County
Waterfowl: Varied Species of ducks, Canada Goose (*Geese*), Whistling Swans

Martin National Wildlife Refuge
Blackwater National Wildlife Refuge
Route 1, Box 121, Cambridge, Maryland 21613
Location: Southwestern States, Maryland
Waterfowl: Varied Species of ducks, Canada Goose (*Geese*)

Massachusetts:

Pond Island National Wildlife Refuge
Parker River National Wildlife Refuge
Newburyport, Massachusetts 01950
Location: on the Atlantic, Northeastern States of Portland
Waterfowl: Sea Ducks, Common Eider Ducks

Rachel Carson National Wildlife Refuge
Parker River National Wildlife Refuge
Newburyport, Massachusetts 01950
Location: A 45 mile stretch from Kittery to south of Portland
Waterfowl: Green-Winged Teal, Canada Goose (*Geese*), Black Ducks

Northeastern States
Massachusetts, continued:

Great Meadows National Wildlife Refuge
191 Sudbury Road, Concord, Massachusetts 01742
Location: One section north and one south of Concord, approximately 20 miles west of Boston
Waterfowl: Wood Ducks, Teal, Mallards, Canada Goose (*Geese*)

Monomoy National Wildlife Refuge
Great Meadows National Wildlife Refuge
191 Sudbury Road, Concord, Massachusetts 01742
Location: East Massachusett, one the Cape, just south of chatham
Waterfowl: Green-Wing Teal, Scoters, Black Ducks, Common Eider Ducks, Canada Goose (*Geese*)

Nantucket National Wildlife Refuge
Great Meadows National Wildlife Refuge
191 Sudbury Road, Concord, Massachusetts 07142
Location: North Nantucket Island, south of Cape Cod
Waterfowl: Migratory Sea Ducks, Black Ducks, Canada Goose (*Geese*)

Parker River National Wildlife Refuge
Newburyport, Massachusetts 01950
Location: Northeastern States, Massachusetts, 35 miles north of Boston
Waterfowl: Green-Winged Teal, Black Ducks, Canada Goose (*Geese*)

New Jersey:

Brigantine National Wildlife Refuge
P.O. Box 72, Oceanville, New Jersey 08231
Location: Coastal New Jersey, off U.S. Route 9, just north of Atlantic City
Waterfowl: Black Ducks, Gadwalls, Pintails, Shovelers, Canada Goose (*Geese*), Brant, Mute Swans, Lesser Snow Goose (*Geese*)

Great Samp National Wildlife Refuge
R.D. 1, Box 148, Basking Ridge, New Jersey 07920
Location: Headquarters on Pleasant Plains road, North New Jersey
Waterfowl: Varied species of ducks, Canada Goose (*Geese*)

New York:

Iroquois National Wildlife Refuge
Basom, New York 14013
Location: West, New York
Waterfowl: Black Ducks, Mallards, Pintails, Widgeons (*Wigeons*), Canada Goose (*Geese*)

Montezuma National Wildlife Refuge
R.D. 1, Box 1411, Seneca Falls, New York 13148
Location: Central New York, just east of Seneca Falls
Waterfowl: Wood Ducks, Blue-Winged Teal, Mallards, Canada Goose (*Geese*)

Morton Wildlife Refuge
RD 359, Noyack Road, Sag Harbor, New York 11963

Location: East Long Island
Waterfowl: Black Ducks, American Goldeneyes, Red-Breasted Mergansers, Old Squaws

Pennsylvania:

Erie National Wilflife Refuge
R.D. 2, Box 167, Guys Mills, Pennsylvania
Pennsylvania:
Erie National Wildlife Refuge
R.D. 2, Box 167, Guys Mills, Pennsylvania 16327
Location: Northwestern Pennsylvania, entrance on State Route 173, just south of Mt. Hope
Waterfowl: Varied species of ducks, Canada Goose (*Geese*)

Middle Creek Wildlife Management Area
R.D. 1, Newmanstown, Pennsylvania 17073
Location: East Pennsylvania
Waterfowl: Wood Ducks, Mallards, Canada Goose (*Geese*), Swans

Pymatuning Waterfowl Area
R.D. 1, Hartstown, Pennsylvania 16131
Location: Northwestern, Pennsylvania, just south of Linesville
Waterfowl: Black Ducks, Wood Ducks, Mallards, Blue-Winged Teal, Gadwalls, Canada Goose (*Geese*)

Tinicum National Environmental Center
Suite 104, Scott Plaza 2, Philadelphia, Pennsylvania 19113
Location: Near International Airport
Waterfowl: Black Ducks, Pintails, Green-Winged Teal, Blue-Winged Teal, Widgeons (*Wigeons*), Ruddy Ducks, American Mergansers, Mallards, Canada Goose (*Geese*)

Rhode Island:

Sachuset Point National Wildlife Refuge
Ninigret National Wildlife Refuge
Box 307, Charleston, Rhode Island 02813
Location: Southeastern States, Aquidneck Island, just east of Newport
Waterfowl: Black Ducks, Gadwalls, Mallards, Blue-Winged Teal, Pintails, Buffleheads, Common Eider Ducks, Old Squaws, Scoters, Ruddy Ducks

Trustom Pond National Wildlife Refuge
Ninigret National Wildlife Refuge, Box 307, Charleston, Rhode Island 02813
Location: South coast, near Wakefiled
Waterfowl: Black Ducks, Pintails, Mallards, Blue-Winged Teal, Canvasbacks, Redheads, Great Scaup, Ruddy Ducks, Canada Goose (*Goose*)

Vermont:

Missiquoi National Wildlife Refuge
Swanton, Vermont 05488
Location: Northwestern, Vermont, on State Route 78
Waterfowl: Wood Ducks, American Goldeneyes, Canada Goose (*Geese*)

Virginia:

Buckbay National Wildlife Refuge
Box 6128, Virginia Beach, Virginia 23456
Location: Southeastern States, Virginia, near Virginia Beach
Waterfowl: Canada Goose (*Geese*), Lesser Snow Goose (*Geese*), Whistling Swans

Chincoteague National Wildlife Refuge
P.O. Box 62, Chincoteague, Virginia 23336
Location: Northeastern States, Virginia, also southern Maryland
Waterfowl: Varied species of ducks, Canada Goose (*Geese*), Lesser Scaup, Whistling Swans

Mason Neck National Wildlife Refuge
P.O. Box A, Woodbridge, Virginia 22191
Location: Northeastern States, Virginia, just south of Washington, D.C.
Waterfowl: Black Ducks, Mallards, Wood Ducks, Lesser Scaup, Canada Goose (*Geese*), Whistling Swans

Presquile National Wildlife Refuge
P.O. Box 658, Hopewell, Virginia 23860
Location: Southeastern States, Virginia
Waterfowl: Puddle Ducks, Canada Goose (*Geese*), Lesser Snow Goose (*Geese*)

Southeastern States
Alabama:

Choctaw National Wildlife Refuge
Box 325, Jackson, Alabama 36545
Location: Southwestern, Alabama
Waterfowl: Black Ducks, Mallards, Pintails, Wood Ducks, varied other species of ducks

Eufaula National Wildlife Refuge
Box 258, Eufaula, Alabama 36027
Location: Southeastern, Alabama, and into Georgia
Waterfowl: Mallards, Widgeons, (*Wigeons*), Ring-Necked Ducks, Canada Goose (*Geese*), Lesser Snow Goose (*Geese*)

Wheeler National Refuge
Box 1643, Decatur, Alabama 35601
Location: North Alabama
Waterfowl: Varied species of ducks, Canada Goose (*Geese*)

Arkansas:

Big Lake National Wildlife Refuge
P.O. Box 57, Manila, Arkansas 72442
Location: Northeastern, Arkansas
Waterfowl: Wood Ducks, Mallards, Hooded Mergansers

Holla Bend National Wildlife Refuge
P.O. Box 1043, Russellville, Arkansas 72801
Location: Central Arkansas
Waterfowl: Mallards, Gadwalls, Pintails, Widgeons (*Wigeons*), Green-Winged Teal, Canada Goose (*Geese*)

Wapanocca National Wildlife Refuge
P.O. Box 257, Turrell, Arkansas 72384
Location: Eastcentral, Arkansas, just west of the Mississippi River

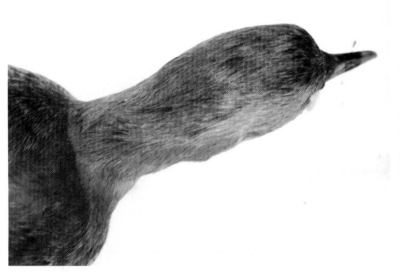

Pied-Billed Grebe, top of head and bill detail

Back feather detail, note streaked appearance of feathers

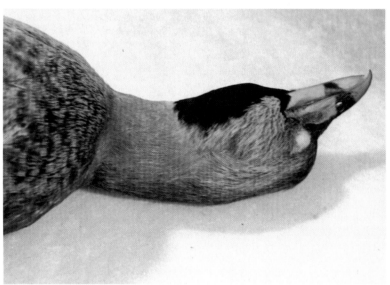

Side of head, bill detail and chest

Back, note feather pattern on this specimen

Side and belly, note belly not pure white

Close-up of rump and feet

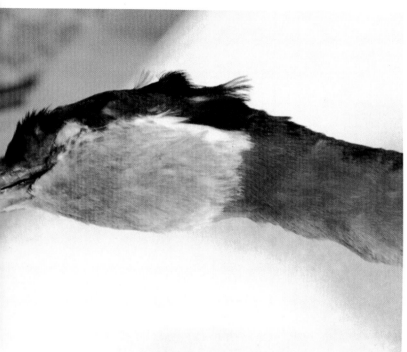

Underneath head and neck of Red-Necked Grebe

Head and bill detail

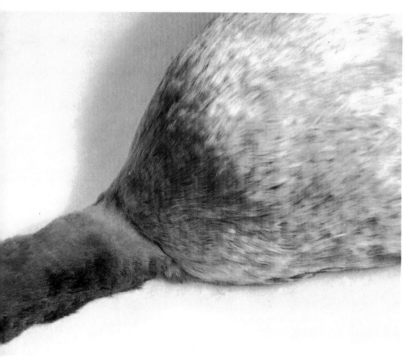

Neck and chest, note color of both

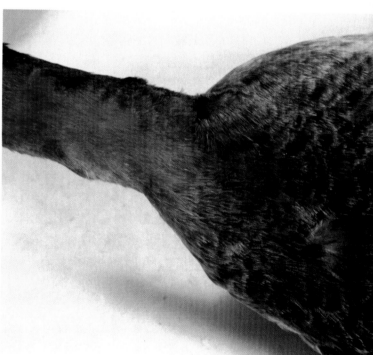

Upper back and neck feather detail

Waterfowl: Wood Ducks, Mallards, Hooded Mergansers

White River National Refuge
P.O. Box 308, DeWitt, Arkansas 72042
Location: Southeastern, Arkansas
Waterfowl: Black Ducks, Mallards, Gadwalls, Pintails, Green-Winged Teal, Widgeons (*Wigeons*), Shovelers, Wood Ducks, Ring-Necked Ducks, Lesser Scaup, Canada Goose (*Geese*)

Georgia:

Harris Neck National Wildlife Refuge
Route 1, Hardeeville, South Carolina 29927
Location: Coastal Georgia, along State Route 131
Waterfowl: Varied species of ducks, Canada Goose (*Geese*)

Okefenokee National Wildlife Refuge
P.O. Box 117, Waycross, Georgia 31501
Location: Southeastern, Georgia, near the Florida border
Waterfowl: Wood Ducks, varied other species of ducks

Savannah National Wildlife Refuge
Location: Southeastern, Georgia
Waterfowl: Black Ducks, Gadwalls, Pintails, Green-Winged Teal, Mallards, Ring-Necked Ducks, Wood Ducks

Florida:

Chassahowitzka National Wildlife Refuge
Route 1, Box 153, Homosassa, Florida 32646
Location: The Gulf Coast of Florida, on U.S. 19
Waterfowl: Black Ducks, Mallards, Gadwalls, Pintails, Widgeons (*Wigeons*), Redheads, Canvasbacks

J. N. Ding Darling National Wildlife Refuge
P.O. Drawer B, Sanibel, Florida 33957
Location: Just off the southwestern coast of Florida
Waterfowl: Pintails, Lesser Scaup, Red-Breasted Merganser

Lake Woodruff National Wildlife Refuge
P.O. Box 448, Deleon Springs, Florida 32028
Location: East coast of Route 40-A
Waterfowl: Pintails, Wood Ducks, Green-Winged Teal, Ring-Necked Ducks, Scaup

Loxahatchee National Wildlife Refuge
Box 278, Delray Beach, Florida 33444
Location: Southeastern, Florida, just west of Delray Beach
Waterfowl: Wood Ducks, Ring-Necked Ducks, Pintails, Green-Winged Teal, Blue-Winged Teal, Widgeons (*Wigeons*), Shovelers

Merritt Island National Wildlife Refuge
P.O. Box 6504, Titusville, Florida 32780
Location: Atlantic coast of south Florida, on State Route 402
Waterfowl: Gadwalls, Pintails, Lesser Scaup, Teal

St. Markes National Wildlife Refuge
P.O. Box 68, St. Markes, Florida 32355
Locations: Northwestern, Gulf Coast of Florida
Waterfowl: Pintails, Widgeons (*Wigeons*), Redheads, Ring-Necked Ducks, Buffleheads, Canada Goose (*Geese*)

Louisiana:

Breton National Wildlife Refuge
Delta-Breton Islands National Wildlife Refuge
Pilottown, Louisiana 70053
Location: Northeastern, Mississippi River Delta
Waterfowl: Black Ducks, Redheads, Scaup, Widgeons (*Wigeons*), Buffleheads

Delta National Wildlife Refuge
Venice, Louisiana 70091
Location: East Bank of the Mississippi River
Waterfowl: Gadwalls, Pintails, Widgeons (*Wigeons*), Green-Winged Teal, Shovelers, Lesser Snow Goose (*Geese*)

Lacassine National Wildlife Refuge
Route 1, Box 186, Lake Arthur, Louisiana 70549
Location: South Louisiana on State Route 3056
Waterfowl: Fulvous Whistling Ducks (*Fulvous Tree Duck*), Mallards, Gadwalls, Pintails, Green-Winged Teal, Blue-Winged Teal, Widgeons (*Wigeons*), Shovelers, Rig-Necked Ducks, Lesser Scaup, Ruddy Ducks, Hooded Mergansers, Canada Goose (*Geese*), White-Fronted Goose (*Geese*), Lesser Snow Goose (*Geese*)

Sabine National Wildlife Refuge
MRH Box 107, Hackberry, Louisiana 70645
Location: Southwestern, Louisiana
Waterfowl: Black Ducks, Mallards, Widgeons (*Wigeons*), Pintails, Green-Winged Teal, Blue-Winged Teal, Shovelers, Lesser Scaup, Lesser Snow Goose (*Geese*)

Mississippi:

Noxubee National Wildlife Refuge
Route 1, Brookesville, Mississippi 39739
Location: Eastcentral States, Mississippi
Waterfowl: Gadwalls, Green-Winged Teal, Mallards, Widgeons (*Wigeons*), Wood Ducks, Ring-Necked Ducks

Yazoo National Wildlife Refuge
Route 1, Box 286, Hollandale, Mississippi 38748
Location: West Mississippi, approximately half-hour south of Greenville
Waterfowl: Black Ducks, Mallards, Gadwalls, Pintails, Green-Winged Teal, Widgeons (*Wigeons*), Shovelers, Ring-Necked Ducks, Wood Ducks

North Carolina:

Mattamuskeet National Wildlife Refuge
New Holland, North Carolina 27885
Location: East North Carolina, approximately half-hour south of Columbia
Waterfowl: Black Ducks, Mallards, Pintails, Canada Goose (*Geese*), Lesser Snow Goose (*Geese*), Whistling Swans

Pea Island National Wildlife Refuge
P.O. Box 1026, Manteo, North Carolina 27954
Location: The Outer Banks on Hatteras Island
Waterfowl: Varied species of ducks, Canada Goose (*Geese*), Lesser Snow Goose (*Geese*) and Whistling Swans

Pungo National Wildlife Refuge
P.O. Box 116, Plymouth, North Carolina 27962
Location: East North Carolina
Waterfowl: Black Ducks, Mallards, Pintails, Canada Goose (*Geese*)

Swanquarter National Wildlife Refuge
New Holland, North Carolina 27885
Location: Coastal North Carolina
Waterfowl: Black Ducks, Mallards, Pintails, Canada Goose (*Geese*), Whistling Swans

South Carolina:

Cape Romaine National Wildlife Refuge
Route 1, Box 191, Awendaw, South Carolina 29429
Location: Moore's Landing on See Wee Road
Waterfowl: Black Ducks, Gadwalls, Teal, Ring-Necked Ducks, Scaup, Buffleheads, Canada Goose (*Geese*)

Carolina Sandhills National Wildlife Refuge
McBee, South Carolina 29101
Location: Northeastern, South Carolina
Waterfowl: Black Ducks, Mallard, Wood Ducks, Canada Goose (*Geese*)

Santee National Wildlife Refuge
P.O. Box 158, Summerton, South Carolina 29148
Location: Southcentral States, South Carolina
Waterfowl: Varied species of ducks, Canada Goose (*Geese*)

Tennessee:

Cross Creeks National Wildlife Refuge
Route 1, Box 113-B, Dover, Tennessee 37058
Location: Northwestern, Tennessee, several miles from Dover
Waterfowl: Wood Ducks, Canada Goose (*Geese*)

Hatchie National Wildlife Refuge
Box 127, Brownsville, Tennessee 37058
Location: West Tennessee
Waterfowl: Wood Ducks, Mallards, various other ducks

Reelfoot National Wildlife Refuge
Box 295, Samburg, Tennessee 38254
Location: Northwestern, Tennessee
Waterfowl: varied other species of ducks, Mallards, Pintails, Ring-Necked Ducks, Canada Goose (*Geese*)

Tennessee National Wildlife Refuge
P.O. Box 849, Paris
Tennessee 38242

Pacific States
California

Clear Lake National Wildlife Refuge
Route 1, Box 74, Tulelake, California 96134
Location: North California in the Klamath Basin
Pintails, Mallards, Green-Winged Teal, Cinnamon Teal, Shovelers, Widgeons (*Wigeons*), Redheads, Lesser Scaup, Ruddy Ducks, American Mergansers, Canada Goose (*Geese*), Lesser Snow Goose (*Geese*), Whistling Swans

Kern National Wildlife Refuge
P.O. Box 219, Delano, California 93215
Location: South California
Waterfowl: Pintails, Mallards, Gadwalls, Green-Winged Teal, Cinnamon Teal, Shovelers, Widgeons (*Wigeons*), Ruddy Ducks, Canada Goose (*Geese*), White-Fronted Goose (*Geese*)

Lower Klamath National Wildlife National Refuge
Route 1, Box 74, Tulelake, California 96134
Location: North California
Waterfowl: Pintails, Mallards, Green-Winged Teal, Cinnamon Teal, Shovelers, Widgeons (*Wigeons*), Redheads, Lesser Scaup, Ruddy Ducks, American Mergansers, Canada Goose (*Geese*), White-Fronted Goose (*Geese*), Lesser Snow Goose (*Geese*), Whistling Swans

Merced National Wildlife Refuge
P.O. Box 2176, Los Banos, California 93625
Location: Central California, in the San Joaquin Valley
Waterfowl: Pintails, Mallards, Green-Winged Teal, Shovelers, Widgeons (*Wigeons*), Canada Goose (*Geese*), White-Fronted Goose (*Geese*), Lesser Snow Goose (*Geese*), Whistling Swans

Modoc National Wildlife Refuge
P.O. Box 111, Lakeview, Oregon 97630
Location: Northeastern States, california
Waterfowl: Pintails, Mallards, Gadwalls, Green-Winged Teal, Cinnamon Teal, Shovelers, Widgeons (*Wigeons*), Lesser Scaup, American Goldeneyes, Buffleheads, Ruddy Ducks, American Mergansers, Canada Goose (*Geese*), White-Fronted Goose (*Geese*), Lesser Snow Goose (*Geese*), Whistling Swans

Pixley National Wildlife Refuge
P.O. Box 219, Delano, California 93215
Location: South California
Waterfowl: Pintails, Mallards, Green-Winged Teal, Shovelers, Widgeons (*Wigeons*), Ruddy Ducks, Canada Goose (*Geese*), White-Fronted Goose (*Geese*), Lesser Snow Goose (*Geese*), Whistling Swans

Sacramento National Wildlife Refuge
Route 1, Box 311, Willows, California 95988
Location: North California, on U. S. 99W
Waterfowl: Pintails, Mallards, Green-Winged Teal, Shovelers, Widgeons (*Wigeons*), Ruddy Ducks, Canada Goose

(*Geese*), White-Fronted Goose (*Geese*), Lesser Snow Goose (*Geese*), Whistling Swans

Salton Sea National Wildlife Refuge
P.O. Box 247, Calipatria, California 92233
Location: South California
Waterfowl: Pintails, Green-Winged Teal, Cinnamon Teal, Shovelers, Widgeons (*Wigeons*), Lesser Scaup, Ruddy Ducks, Canada Goose (*Geese*), Lesser Snow Goose (*Geese*)

San Francisco National Wildlife Refuge
3849 Peralta Boulevard, Suite D, Fremont, California 94536
Location: South San Francisco Bay
Waterfowl: Pintails, Mallards, Gadwalls, Cinnamon Teal, Widgeons (*Wigeons*), Shovelers, Canvasbacks, Greater Scaup, Lesser Scaup, Buffleheads, Surf Scoters, Ruddy Ducks

San Luis National Wildlife Refuge
P.O. Box 2176, Los Banos, California 93635
Location: Central California, in the San Joaquin Valley
Waterfowl: Pintails, Mallards, Green-Winged Teal, Widgeons (*Wigeons*), Shovelers, Canada Goose (*Geese*), White-Fronted Goose (*Geese*), Lesser Snow Goose (*Geese*), Ross Geese

Wildlife Refuge
Pacific States
California
San Pablo Bay National Wildlife Refuge
3849 Peralta Boulevard, Suite D, Fremont, California 94536
Location: North of San Francisco
Waterfowl: Pintails, Mallards, Shovelers, Widgeons (*Wigeons*), Redheads, Canvasbacks, Buffleheads, Ruddy Ducks, Scaup, Scoters

Tulelake National Wildlife Refuge
Route 1, Box 74, Tulelake, California 96134
Location: North California, in the Klamath Basin
Waterfowl: Pintails, Mallards, Green-Winged Teal, Cinnamon Teal, Shovelers, Widgeons (*Wigeons*), Redheads, Lesser Scaup, American Mergansers, Ruddy Ducks, Canada Goose (*Geese*), White-Fronted Goose (*Geese*), Lesser Snow Goose (*Geese*), Whistling Swans

Idaho:

Bear Lake National Wildlife Refuge
802 Washington, Montpelier, Idaho 83254
Location: Southeastern States, Idaho
Waterfowl: Pintails, Mallards, Gadwalls,
Waterfowl: Pintails, Mallards, Gadwalls, Green-Winged Teal, Blue-Winged Teal, Cinnamon Teal, Shovelers, Widgeons (*Wigeons*), Redheads, Canada Goose (*Geese*)

Camas National Wildlife Refuge
Hamer, Idaho 83425
Location: East Idaho
Waterfowl: Pintails, Mallards, Gadwalls, Green-Winged Teal, Blue-Winged Teal,

Cinnamon Teal, Shovelers, Widgeons (*Wigeons*), Redheads, Lesser Scaup, Canvasbacks, American Goldeneyes, Buffleheads, Ruddy Ducks, Canada Goose (*Geese*), Whistling Swans

Deer Flat National Wildlife Refuge
P.O. Box 837, Soda Springs, Idaho 83276
Location: Southeastern, Idaho
Waterfowl: Green-Winged Teal, Blue-Winged Teal, Cinnamon Teal, Shovelers, Widgeons (*Wigeons*), Redheads, Buffleheads, Ruddy Ducks, Canada Goose (*Geese*)

Kootenai National Wildlife Refuge
Route 1, Box 88, Bonners Ferry, Idaho 83805
Location: Idaho
Waterfowl: Pintails, Mallards, Green-Winged Teal, Blue-Winged Teal, Cinnamon Teal, Wood Ducks, American Goldeneyes, Canada Goose (*Geese*), Whistling Swans

Pacific States
Nevada:

Pahranagat National Wildlife Refuge
1500 North Decatur Boulevard, Las Vegas, Nevada 891089
Location: South Nevada
Waterfowl: Pintails, Mallards, Gadwalls, Green-Winged Teal, Canvasbacks

Ruby Lake National Wildlife Refuge
Ruby Valley, Nevada 89833
Location: Northeastern States, Nevada
Waterfowl: Pintails, Mallards, Gadwalls, Green-Winged Teal, Cinnamon Teal, Shovelers, Widgeons (*Wigeons*), Redheads, Ring-Necked Ducks, Canvasbacks, Lesser Scaup, American Goldeneyes, Buffleheads, Ruddy Ducks, Canada Goose (*Geese*), Whistling Swans

Stillwater National Wildlife Refuge
Box 592, Fallon, Nevada 89406
Location: Fallon, Nevada
Waterfowl: Pintails, Mallards, Gadwalls, Green-Winged Teal, Cinnamon Teal, Shovelers, Widgeons (*Wigeons*), Redheads, Canvasbacks, Ruddy Ducks, Canada Goose (*Geese*), American Mergansers, Lesser Snow Goose (*Geese*), Whistling Swans

Oregon:

Ankeny National Wildlife Refuge
Route 1, Box 198, Jefferson, Oregon 97352
Location: Northwestern States, Oregon in the Willamette Valley
Waterfowl: Pintails, Mallards, Green-Winged Teal, Widgeons (*Wigeons*), Shovelers, Wood Ducks, Canada Goose (*Geese*), Whistling Swans

Minidoka National Wildlife Refuge
Route 4, Rupert, Idaho 83350
Location: Southcentral States, Idaho
Waterfowl: Pintails, Mallards, Gadwalls, Green-Winged Teal, Widgeons (*Wigeons*), Ring-Necked Ducks, Redheads, Canvasbacks, Lesser Scaup, American Goldeneyes, American Mergansers, Ruddy Ducks, Canada Goose (*Geese*), Whistling Swans

Western Grebe neck, long and thin

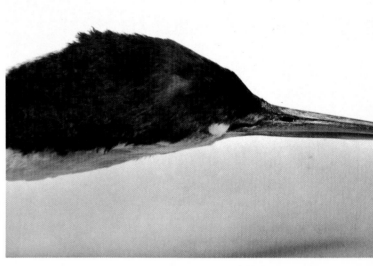

Head and bill, note bill detail

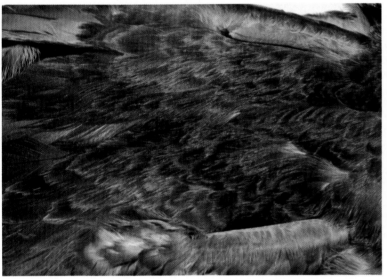

Back feather detail

Detail of tertials and primaries

Upper back feather detail

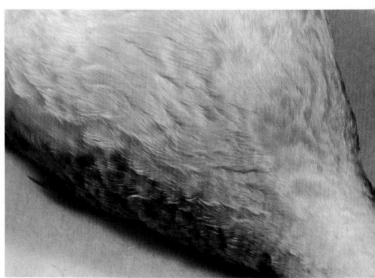

Underneath chest detail

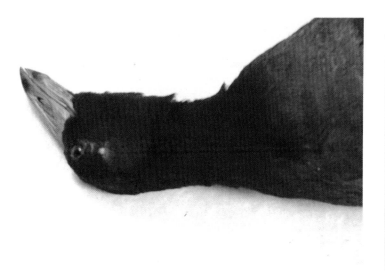

American Coot head, note bill detail

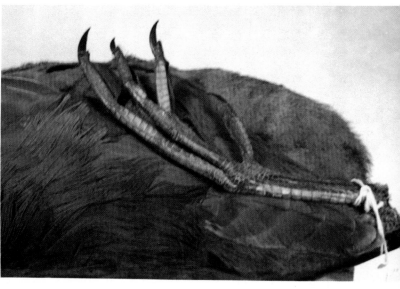

Side, note large, clawed feet

American Coot

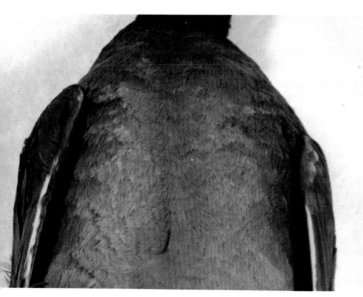

nderneath chest detail

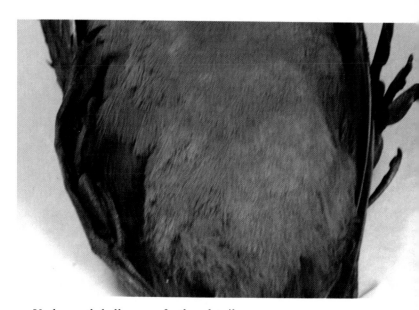

Underneath belly area, feather detail

ck of Coot

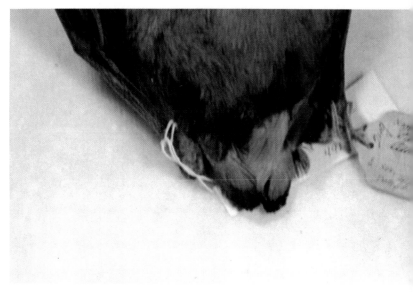

Underneath rump area, note small tail

William L. Finley National Wildlife Refuge
Route 2, Box 208, Corvallis, Oregon 97330
Location: Northwestern States, Oregon on State Route 99W
Waterfowl: Pintails, Green-Winged Teal, Shovelers, Widgeons (*Wigeons*), Wood Ducks, Canada Goose (*Geese*), Whistling Swans

Klamath Forest National Wildlife Refuge
Route 1, Box 74, Tululake, California 96134
Location: South Oregon
Waterfowl: Pintails, Mallards, Green-Winged Teal, Cinnamon Teal, Shovelers, Widgeons (*Wigeons*), Redheads, Lesser Scaup, American Mergansers, Ruddy Ducks, Canada Goose (*Geese*), White-Fronted Goose (*Geese*), Lesser Snow Goose (*Geese*), Whistling Swans

Lewis and Clark National Wildlife Refuge
Route 1, Box 3760, Cathlamet, Washington 98612
Location: Northwestern States, Oregon
Waterfowl: Pintails, Mallards, Green-Winged Teal, Widgeons (*Wigeons*), Canada Goose (*Geese*), Whistling Swans

Malheur National Wildlife Refuge
P.O. Box 113, Burns, Oregon 97720
Location: Southeastern, Oregon
Waterfowl: Pintails, Mallards, Gadwalls, Green-Winged Teal, Cinnamon Teal, Shovelers, Widgeons (*Wigeons*), Redheads, Canvasbacks, Lesser Scaup, American Goldeneyes, Bufflehead, Ruddy Ducks, American Mergansers, Canada Goose (*Geese*), Lesser Snow Goose (*Geese*), Whistling Swans

Umatilla National Wildlife Refuge
Box 239, Umatilla, Oregon 97882
Location: Northcentral States, Oregon
Waterfowl: Pintails, Mallards, Green-Winged Teal, Widgeons (*Wigeons*), American Goldeneyes, Buffleheads, Canada Goose (*Geese*), Whistling Swans

Baskett Slough National Wildlife Refuge
Route 1, Box 709, Dallas, Oregon 97338
Location: Northwestern States, Oregon in the Willamette Valley
Waterfowl: Pintails, Mallards, Green-Winged Teal, Shovelers, Widgeons (*Wigeons*), Wood Ducks, Canada Goose (*Geese*), Whistling Swans

Hart Mountain National Wildlife Refuge
P.O. Box 111, Lakeview, Oregon 97630
Location: Southcentral States, Oregon
Waterfowl: Pintails, Mallards, Gadwalls, Green-Winged Teal, Cinnamon Teal, Shovelers, Widgeons (*Wigeons*), Redheads, Canvasbacks, Ruddy Ducks, Buffleheads, American Mergansers, Canada Goose (*Geese*), Whistling Swans

Washington:

Columbia National Wildlife Refuge
44 S. 8th Avenue, Othello, Washington 99344
Location: Southwestern, Washington
Waterfowl: Mallards, Pintails,

Green-Winged Teal, Blue-Winged Teal, Cinnamon Teal, Ring-Necked Ducks, Widgeons (*Wigeons*), Lesser Scaup, American Goldeneyes, Ruddy Ducks, Buffleheads, Canada Goose (*Geese*)

Columbian White Tailed Deer National Wildlife Refuge
Route 1, Box 3760, Cathlamet, Washington 98612
Location: Southwestern States, Washington
Waterfowl: Pintails, Mallards, Widgeons (*Wigeons*), Canada Goose (*Geese*), Whistling Swans

McNary National Wildlife Refuge
Box 308, Burbank, Washington 99323
Location: Southwestern States, Washington
Waterfowl: Pintails, Mallards, Widgeons (*Wigeons*), Green-Winged Teal, Blue-Winged Teal, Cinnamon Teal, Shovelers, Gadwalls, Ring-Necked Ducks, Redheads, Canvasbacks, Lesser Scaup, American Goldeneyes, Barrow's Goldeneyes, Buffleheads, Ruddy Ducks, American Mergansers, Canada Goose (*Geese*), Whistling Swans

Ridgefield National Wildlife Refuge
P.O. Box 457, Ridgefield, Washington 98642
Location: Northwestern, Washington
Waterfowl: Pintails, Mallards, Green-Winged Teal, Cinnamon Teal, Shovelers, Widgeons (*Wigeons*), Canada Goose (*Geese*), Whistling Swans

Toppenish National Wildlife Refuge
Route 1, Box 1300, Toppenish, Washington 98948
Location: Southcentral States, Washington
Waterfowl: Pintails, Mallards, Green-Winged Teal, Cinnamon Teal, Shovelers, Widgeons (*Wigeons*), Wood Ducks, Canada Goose (*Geese*)

Turnbull National Wildlife Refuge
Route 3, Box 385, Cheyney, Washington 99004
Location: East Washington
Waterfowl: Mallards, Pintails, Gadwalls, Green-Winged Teal, Blue-Winged Teal, Cinnamon Teal, Shovelers, Widgeons (*Wigeons*), Redheads, Lesser Scaup, American Goldeneyes, Buffleheads, Ruddy Ducks, Canada Goose (*Geese*), Whistling Swans, Trumpeter Swans

Willapa National Wildlife Refuge
Ilwaco, Washington 98624
Location: Southwestern, Washington
Waterfowl: Pintails, Mallards, Gadwalls, Green-Winged Teal, Brant, Widgeons (*Wigeons*), Wood Ducks, Canvasbacks, Greater Scaup, Buffleheads, Scoters, Canada Goose (*Geese*), Whistling Swans, Trumpeter Swans

Southwestern States
Arizona:

Cibola National Wildlife Refuge
P.O. Box AP, Blythe, California 92225
Location: Lower Colorado River, Arizona,

and the Palo Verde Valley, California
Waterfowl: Pintails, Mallards, Canada Goose (*Geese*)

Havasu National Wildlife Refuge
P.O. Box A, Needles, California 92363
Location: West Arizona, and Southeastern States, California
Waterfowl: Pintails, Mallards, Gadwalls, Green-Winged Teal, Cinnamon Teal, Shovelers, Widgeons (*Wigeons*), Redheads, Ruddy Ducks, Canada Goose (*Geese*), Lesser Snow Goose (*Geese*)

Imperial National Wildlife Refuge
P.O. Box 2217, Martinez Lake, Arizona 85364
Location: 30 miles along the Colorado River on the California and Arizona sides

New Mexico:

Bitter Lake National Wildlife Refuge
P.O. Box 7, Rosewell, New Mexico 88201
Location: Southeastern States, New Mexico
Waterfowl: Pintails, Mallards, Gadwalls, Shovelers, Widgeons (*Wigeons*), Ruddy Ducks, Canada Goose (*Geese*), Lesser Snow Goose (*Geese*)

Bosque Del Apache National Wildlife Refuge
P.O. Box 278, San Antonio, New Mexico 87832
Location: Along the Rio Grande River
Waterfowl: Pintails, Mallards, Gadwalls, Green-Winged Teal, Shovelers, Widgeons (*Wigeons*), Canada Goose (*Geese*), Lesser Snow Goose (*Geese*)

Las Vegas National Wildlife Refuge
P.O. Box 1070, Las Vegas, New Mexico 87701
Location: Northeastern States, New Mexico
Waterfowl: Pintails, Mallards, Gadwalls, Green-Winged Teal, Blue-Winged Teal, Cinnamon Teal, Shovelers, Widgeons (*Wigeons*), Ring-Necked Ducks, Canvasbacks, Green-Winged Teal, Lesser Scaup, American Goldeneyes, Buffleheads, American Mergansers, Ruddy Ducks, Canada Goose (*Geese*)

Maxwell National Wildlife Refuge
P.O. Box 1070, Las Vegas, New Mexico
Location: Northeastern States, New Mexico
Waterfowl: Pintails, Mallards, Gadwalls, Blue-Winged Teal, Green-Winged Teal, Shovelers, Widgeons (*Wigeons*), Redheads, Lesser Scaup, Buffleheads, American Mergansers, Ruddy Ducks, Canada Goose (*Geese*)

Oklahoma:

Salt Plains National Wildlife Refuge
Jest, Oklahoma
Location: North Oklahoma
Waterfowl: Pintails, Mallards, Green-Winged Teal, Canada Goose (*Geese*), Lesser Snow Goose (*Geese*), Whited-Fronted Goose (*Geese*)

Sequoyah National Wildlife Refuge
P.O. Box 398, Sallisaw, Oklahoma
Location: Eastcentral States, Oklahoma
Waterfowl: Pintails, Mallards, Gadwalls,
Green-Winged Teal, Widgeons (*Wigeons*),
Canvasbacks, Redheads, Scaup

Tishomingo National Wildlife Refuge
P.O. Box 248, Tishomingo, Oklahoma
73460
Location: Southeastern States, Oklahoma
Waterfowl: Pintails, Mallards, Gadwalls,
Green-Winged Teal, Shovelers, Widgeons
(*Wigeons*), Wood Ducks, American Mergansers, Lesser Scaup, Canada Goose
(*Geese*), White-Fronted Goose (*Geese*)

Washita National Wildlife Refuge
R.R. 1, Box 68, Butler, Oklahoma 73625
Location: West Oklahoma
Waterfowl: Pintails, Mallards, Widgeons
(*Wigeons*), Canada Goose (*Geese*), White-
Fronted Goose (*Geese*)

Wichita Mountains Wildlife Refuge
P.O. Box 448, Cache, Oklahoma 73527
Location: Southwestern States, Oklahoma
Waterfowl: Mallards, Gadwalls, Widgeons
(*Wigeons*), Ring-Necked Ducks, Redheads

Texas:

Anahuac National Wildlife Refuge
P.O. Box 278, Anahuac, Texas 77514
Location: Southeastern States, Texas
Waterfowl: Pintails, Widgeons (*Wigeons*),
Teal, Canada Goose (*Geese*), White-Front-
ed Goose (*Geese*)

Aransas National Wildlife Refuge
P.O. Box 68, Austwell, Texas 77950
Location: Gulf of Mexico
Waterfowl: Pintails, Gadwalls, Blue-
Winged Teal, Shovelers, Lesser Scaup,
Canada Goose (*Geese*)

Brazoria National Wildlife Refuge
P.O. Box 1088, Angleton, Texas 77515
Location: Gulf of Mexico
Waterfowl: Pintails, Gadwalls, Green-
Winged Teal, Canada Goose (*Geese*),
Lesser Snow Goose (*Geese*)

Buffalo Lake National Wildlife Refuge
Box 228, Umbarger, Texas 79091
Location: Northwestern States, Texas
Waterfowl: Pintails, Mallards, Gadwalls,
Green-Winged Teal, Blue-Winged Teal,
Shovelers, Widgeons (*Wigeons*), Canada
Goose (*Geese*), Lesser Snow Goose (*Geese*)

Hagerman National Wildlife Refuge
Route 3, Box 123, Sherman, Texas 75090
Location: Northeastern States, Texas
Waterfowl: Mallards, Widgeons
(*Wigeons*), Green-Winged Teal, Canvas-
backs, Redheads, Scaup, Ring-Necked
Ducks, Canada Goose (*Geese*), Lesser Snow
Goose (*Geese*), White-Fronted Goose
(*Geese*)

Laguna Atascosa National Wildlife Refuge
306 East Jackson Street, P.O. Box 2683,
Harlington, Texas 78550
Location: South Texas
Waterfowl: Pintails, Shovelers, Ruddy

Ducks, Redheads, Canada Goose (*Geese*),
Lesser Snow Goose (*Geese*)

Muleshoe National Wildlife Refuge
P.O. Box 549, Muleshoe, Texas 78347
Location: Texas Panhandle
Waterfowl: Pintails, Mallards, Gadwalls,
Green-Winged Teal, Blue-Winged Teal,
Cinnamon Teal, Shovelers, Widgeons
(*Wigeons*), Ring-Necked Ducks, Red-
heads, Canvasbacks, Lesser Scaup, Buffle-
heads, Ruddy Ducks, Canada Goose
(*Geese*), Lesser Snow Goose (*Geese*)

San Bernard National Wildlife Refuge
P.O. Drawer 1088, Angleton, Texas 77515
Location: Gulf of Mexico
Waterfowl: Mallards, Green-Winged Teal,
Blue-Winged Teal, Shovelers, Widgeons
(*Wigeons*), Canada Goose (*Geese*), Lesser
Snow Goose (*Geese*), White-Fronted Goose
(*Geese*)

Santa Ana National Wildlife Refuge
306 East Jackson Street, P.O. Box 2683,
Harlington, Texas 78550
Location: South Texas, on the Mexican
border
Waterfowl: Pintails, Black-Bellied Whist-
ling Ducks, Gadwalls, Blue-Winged Teal,
Cinnamon Teal, Shovelers, Widgeons
(*Wigeons*)

Southcentral States
Colorado:

Alamosa National Wildlife Refuge
P.O. Box 1148, Alamosa, Colorado 81101
Location: Southcentral Colorado, in the
San Luis Valley
Waterfowl: Pintails, Mallards, Gadwalls,
Green-Winged Teal, Blue-Winged Teal,
Cinnamon Teal, Common Mergansers,
Northern Shovelers

Arapaho National Wildlife Refuge
P.O. Box 457, Walden, Colorado 80480
Location: Northern Colorado
Waterfowl: Gadwalls, Mallards, Green-
Winged Teal, Blue-Winged Teal, Lesser
Scaup, Widgeons (*Wigeons*)

Browns Park National Wildlife Refuge
Greystone, Colorado 81636
Location: Northwestern Colorado
Waterfowl: Redheads, Canada Geese

Monte Vista National Wildlife Refuge
Box 511, Monte Vista, Colorado 81144
Location: Southcentral Colorado
Waterfowl: Pintails, Mallards, Gadwalls,
Green-Winged Teal, Blue-Winged Teal,
Cinnamon Teal, Redheads, Northern
Shovelers, Common Mergansers, Canada
Geese

Iowa:

DeSoto National Wildlife Refuge
Route 1-B, Missouri Valley, Iowa 51555
Location: Western Iowa, on U. S. Route
30
Waterfowl: Black Ducks, Mallards, Pin-
tails, Gadwalls, Green-Winged Teal, Blue-
Winged Teal, Widgeons (*Wigeons*),
Northern Shovelers, Ring-Necked Ducks,

Wood Ducks, Lesser Scaup, Buffleheads,
Common Mergansers, Canada Geese,
Snow Geese, White-Fronted Geese

Union Slough National Wildlife Refuge
P.O. Box AF, Titnoka, Iowa 50480
Location: Northcentral Iowa, on the
Eastern edge of the Great Plains
Waterfowl: Black Ducks, Mallards, Pin-
tails, Gadwalls, Green-Winged Teal, Blue-
Winged Teal, Northern Shovelers,
Widgeons (*Wigeons*), Redheads, Wood
Ducks, Ring-Necked Ducks, Canvasbacks,
Ruddy Ducks, Canada Geese, Snow Geese

Kansas:

Flint Hills National Wildlife Refuge
P.O. Box 213, Burlington, Kansas 66839
Location: Eastern Kansas
Waterfowl: Pintails, Mallards, Gadwalls,
Green-Winged Teal, Blue-Winged Teal,
Widgeons (*Wigeons*), Northern Shovelers,
Redheads, Wood Ducks, Ring-Necked
Ducks, Lesser Scaup, Canvasbacks, Com-
mon Mergansers, Canada Geese, Snow
Geese, White-Fronted Geese

Kirwin National Wildlife Refuge
Box 125, Kirwin, Kansas 67644
Location: Northcentral Kansas
Waterfowl: Pintails, Mallards, Green-
Winged Teal, Canada Geese, white-Front-
ed Geese

Quivira National Wildlife Refuge
P.O. Box G, Stafford, Kansas 67578
Location: Central Kansas
Waterfowl: Pintails, Mallards, Green-
Winged Teal, Blue-Winged Teal, North-
ern Shovelers, Widgeons (*Wigeons*), Cana-
da Geese, White-Fronted Geese

Missouri:

Mingo National Wildlife Refuge
R.R. 1, Box 9A, Puxico, Missouri 63960
Location: Southeastern Missouri
Waterfowl: Pintails, Mallards, Gadwalls,
Northern Shovelers, Canada Geese

Squaw Creek National Wildlife Refuge
Box 101, Mound City, Missouri 64470
Location: Northwestern Missouri
Waterfowl: Pintails, Mallards, Canada
Geese, Snow Geese

Swan Lake National Wildlife Refuge
Sumner, Missouri 64681
Location: Northcentral Missouri
Waterfowl: Varied species of ducks,
Canada Geese, Snow Geese

Nebraska:

Crescent Lake National Wildlife Refuge
Star Route, Ellsworth, Nebraska 69340
Location: West Nebraska on the Panhan-
dle
Waterfowl: Pintails, Mallards, Gadwalls,
Green-Winged Teal, Blue-Winged Teal,
Shovelers, Widgeons (*Wigeons*), Ruddy
Ducks, Canada Goose (*Geese*)

Fort Niobrara National Wildlife Refuge
Hidden Timber Road, Valentine, Nebraska

Pair of Fulvous Whistling Ducks

Other Species

Back of the pair

Mandarin Drake, the most colorful duck, note iridescence on front of head

Drake standing with head held close to body, European
Pochards in foreground

Drake walking from water, note high carriage of head

Waterfowl: Pintails, Mallards, Gadwalls, Green-Winged Teal, Blue-Winged Teal, Shovelers, Widgeons (*Wigeons*), Redheads, Ring-Necked Ducks, Lesser Scaup, American Mergansers, Canada Goose (*Geese*)

Valentine National Wildlife Refuge
Valentain, Nebraska 69201
Location: Northcentral States, Nebraska
Waterfowl: Pintails, Mallards, Gadwalls, Green-Winged Teal, Blue-Winged Teal, Shovelers, Widgeons (*Wigeons*), Redheads, Canvasbacks, Buffleheads, Ruddy Ducks, American Mergansers

Utah:

Bear River Migratory Bird Refuge
P.O. Box 459, Brigham City, Utah 84302
Location: Northern Utah on the Bear River delta
Waterfowl: Pintails, Mallards, Gadwalls, Green-Winged Teal, Northern Shovelers, Canvasbacks, Redheads, Ruddy Ducks, Canada Geese, Whistling Swans

Ouray National Wildlife Refuge
447 East Main Street, Suite 4, Vernal, Utah 84078
Location: Northeastern Utah
Waterfowl: Pintails, Mallards, Gadwalls, Blue-Winged Teal, Cinnamon Teal, Ruddy Ducks, Canada Geese

Wyoming:

Hutton Lake National Wildlife Refuge
Arapaho National Wildlife Refuge, P.O. Box 457, Walden, Colorado 80480
Location: Albanie County
Waterfowl: Pintails, Mallards, Gadwalls, Green-Winged Teal, Blue-Winged Teal, Widgeons (*Wigeons*), Shovelers, Redheads, Canvasbacks, Lesser Scaup, Buffleheads, Ruddy Ducks, American Mergansers, Canada Goose (*Geese*)

Seesakadee National Wildlife Refuge
Box 67, Green River, Wyoming 82935
Location: Southwestern States, Wyoming, on the Green River
Waterfowl: Pintails, Mallards, Gadwalls, Green-Winged Teal, Blue-Winged Teal, Widgeons (*Wigeons*), Shovelers, American Goldeneyes, American Mergansers, Canada Goose (*Geese*)

Northcentral States
Montana:

Benton Lake National Wildlife Refuge
P.O. Box 450, Black Eagle, Montana 59414
Location: Northcentral Montana
Waterfowl: Pintails, Gadwalls, Mallards, Green-Winged Teal, Blue-Winged Teal, Widgeons (*Wigeons*), Northern Shoverlers, Snow Geese

Bowdoin National Wildlife Refuge
P. O. Box J, Malta, Montana 59538
Location: Northeastern Montana
Waterfowl: Mallards, Pintails, Gadwalls, Blue-Winged Teal, Widgeons (*Wigeons*), Northern Shovelers, Ruddy Ducks, Canada Geese

Charles M. Russell National Wildlife Refuge
P.O. Box 166, Fort Peck, Montana 59223
Location: Northcentral Montana, along the Missouri River
Waterfowl: Mallards, Pintails, Blue-Winged Teal, Canada Geese

Medicine Lake National Wildlife Refuge
Medicine Lake, Montana 59247
Location: Northeastern Montana
Waterfowl: Mallards, Pintails, Gadwalls, Blue-Winged Teal, Northern Shovelers, Redheads, Canvasbacks, Ruddy Ducks, Canada Geese

Ravalli National Wildlife Refuge
Box 257, Stevensville, Montana 59870
Location: Western Montana
Waterfowl: Wood Ducks, Mallards, Teal, Hooded Mergansers

Red Rock Lake National Wildlife Refuge
Monida Star Route, Box 15, Lima, Montana 59739
Location: Southwestern Montana
Waterfowl: Mallards, Pintails, Gadwalls, Cinnamon Teal, Widgeons (*Wigeons*), Canvasbacks, Lesser Scaup, Canada Geese, Whistling Swans, Trumpeter Swans

North Dakota:

Arrowwood National Wildlife Refuge
Rural route 1, Pingree, North Dakota 58476
Location: Eastern North Dakota
Waterfowl: Mallards, Pintails, Gadwalls, Blue-Winged Teal, Widgeons (*Wigeons*), Wood Ducks, Northern Shovelers, Canada Geese

Audubon National Wildlife Refuge
Rural Route 1, Coleharbor, North Dakota 58531
Location: Westcentral North Dakota
Waterfowl: Mallards, Pintails, Gadwalls,, Green-Winged Teal, Blue-Winged Teal, Widgeons (*Wigeons*), Northern Shovelers, Lesser Scaup, Redheads, Buffleheads, Ruddy Ducks, Common Mergansers, Canada Geese, Snow Geese, white-Fronted Geese

Des Lacs National Wildlife Refuge
Kenmare, North Dakota 58746
Location: Northwestern North dakota
Waterfowl: Mallards, Pintails, Gadwalls, Blue-Winged Teal, Canada Goose (*Geese*), Lesser Snow Goose (*Geese*), White-Fronted Goose (*Geese*)

J. Clark Salyer National Wildlife Refuge
Upham, North Dakota 58789
Location: Northcentral States, North Dakota
Waterfowl: Pintails, Gadwalls, Mallards, Blue-Winged Teal, Widgeons (*Wigeons*), Shovelers, Wood Ducks, Redheads, Canvasbacks, Lesser Scaup, Ruddy Ducks, Canada Goose (*Geese*), Lesser Snow Goose (*Geese*), White-Fronted Goose (*Geese*)

Lake Ilo National Wildlife Refuge
Dunn Center, North Dakota 58626
Location: Western North Dakota

Waterfowl: Pintails, Mallards, Blue-Winged Teal, Shovelers, Gadwalls

Lostwood National Wildlife Refuge
Rural Route 2, Kenmare, North Dakota 58746
Location: Northwestern States, North Dakota
Waterfowl: Pintails, Mallards, Scaup, Teal, Gadwalls, Widgeons (*Wigeons*), Shovelers, Redheads, Canvasbacks

Slade National Wildlife Refuge
Route 1, Cayuga, North Dakota 58013
Location: Southcentral States, North Dakota
Waterfowl: Pintails, Mallards, Gadwalls, Blue-Winged Teal, Shovelers

Tewaukon National Wildlife Refuge
Cayuga, North Dakota 58013
Location: Southeastern North Dakota, on State Route 11
Waterfowl: Pintails, Mallards, Scaup, varied other species of ducks, Snow Geese

Upper Souris National Wildlife Refuge
Foxholm, North Dakota 58738
Location: Northwestern North Dakota
Waterfowl: Pintails, Mallards, Gadwalls, Blue-Winged Teal, Canada Geese, Snow Geese, White-Fronted Geese

South Dakota:

Lacreek National Wildlife Refuge
South Rural Route, Martin, South Dakota 57551
Location: Southwestern South Dakota
Waterfowl: Mallards, Gadwalls, Blue-Winged Teal, Ruddy Ducks, Northern Shovelers, Canada Geese, Trumpeter Swans

Lake Andes National Wildlife Refuge
P.O. Box 279, Lake Andes, South Dakota 57356
Location: Southeastern States, South Dakota
Waterfowl: Pintails, Mallards, Gadwalls, Blue-Winged Teal, Widgeons (*Wigeons*), Lesser Scaup, Canada Goose (*Geese*)

Sand Lake National Wildlife Refuge
Columbia, South Dakota 57433
Location: Northeastern States, South Dakota
Waterfowl: Pintails, Mallards, Gadwalls, Green-Winged Teal, Blue-Winged Teal, Widgeons (*Wigeons*), Shovelers, Redheads, Lesser Scaup, Canada Goose (*Geese*), Lesser Snow Goose (*Geese*)

Waubay National Refuge
R.R. 1, Waubay, South Dakota 57273
Location: Northeastern States, South Dakota
Waterfowl: Mallards, Gadwalls, Lesser Scaup, Blue-Winged Teal, Canada Goose (*Geese*)

Indiana:

Muscatatuck National Wildlife Refuge
P.O. Box 631, Seymour, Indiana 47274
Location: Southcentral Indiana
Waterfowl: Wood Ducks, Canada Geese, Snow Geese

Illinois:

Chautauqua National Wildlife Refuge
Havana, Illinois 62644
Location: Central Illinois, just north of
Havana off Marito Blacktop Road
Waterfowl: Mallards, Wood Ducks, varied
other species of ducks, Canada Geese,
Snow Geese

Crabe Orchard National Wildlife Refuge
P.O. Box J, Carterville, Illinois 62918
Location: Southern Illinois
Waterfowl: Black Ducks, Mallards, Pintails, Gadwalls, Widgeons (*Wigeons*),
Green-Winged Teal, Blue-Winged Teal,
Wood Ducks, Northern Shovelers, Ring-Necked Ducks, Lesser Scaup, Common
Goldeneyes, Buffleheads, Ruddy Ducks,
Hooded Mergansers, Common Mergansers, Canada Geese, Snow Geese

Mark Twain National Wildlife Refuge
P.O. Box 225, Quincy, Illinois 62301
Location: 250 miles of the Mississippi River
in Iowa, Illinois, Missouri
Waterfowl: Black Ducks, Mallards, Pintails, Ring-Necked Ducks, Wood Ducks,
Lesser Scaup, Canada Geese, Snow Geese

Michigan:

Seney National Wildlife Refuge
Seney, Michigan 49883
Location: Upper Peninsula
Waterfowl: Black Ducks, Mallards, Ring-Necked Ducks, Hooded Mergansers, Common Mergansers, Canada Geese, Snow
Geese

Shiawassee National Wildlife Refuge
6975 Mower Road, R.D. 1, Saginaw,
Michigan 48601

Location: Central Lower Peninsula
Waterfowl: Black Ducks, Mallards, Blue-Winged Teal, Canada Geese, Whistling
Swans

Minnesota:

Agassiz National Wildlife Refuge
Middle River, Minnesota 56737
Location: Northwestern Minnesota on
County Road 7
Waterfowl: Mallards, Blue-Winged Teal,
Canada Geese, Whistling Swans

Big Stone National Wildlife Refuge
25 N.W., Second Street, Ortonville,
Minnesota 56278
Location: Western Minnesota
Waterfowl: Mallards, Gadwalls, Pintails,
Green-Winged Teal, Blue-Winged Teal,
Widgeons (*Wigeons*), Northern Shovelers,
Wood Ducks, Redheads, Ring-Necked
Ducks, Lesser Scaup, Canvasbacks, Common Goldeneyes, Ruddy Ducks, Mergansers, Canada Geese, Snow Geese

Rice Lake National Wildlife Refuge
Route 2, McGregor, Minnesota 55760
Location: Northcentral Minnesota
Waterfowl: Black Ducks, Mallards, Wood
Ducks, Widgeons (*Wigeons*), Blue-Winged
Teal, Ring-Necked Ducks, Scaup

Sherburne National Wildlife Refuge
Route 2, Zimmerman, Minnesota 55398
Location: Eastern Minnesota, just southwest of Princeton
Waterfowl: Pintails, Mallards, Blue-Winged Teal, Widgeons (*Wigeons*), Wood
Ducks, Lesser Scaup, Canada Geese

Tamarac National Wildlife Refuge
Rochert, Minnesota 56578

Location: Westcentral Minnesota
Waterfowl: Mallards, Green-Winged Teal,
Blue-Winged Teal, Ring-Necked Ducks,
Common Goldeneyes, Lesser Scaup, Canada Geese

Upper Mississippi River Wildlife and Fish
Refuge
P.O. Box 226, Winona, Minnesota 55987
Location: 284 miles through Minnesota,
Wisconson, Iowa, and Illinois
Waterfowl: Mallards, Gadwalls, Teal,
Wood Ducks, Widgeons (*Wigeons*), Canvasbacks, other diving ducks, Canada
Geese, Whistling Swans

Ohio:

Ottowa National Wildlife Refuge
14000 West State, Route 2, Oak Harbor,
Ohio 43449
Location: Northern Ohio, just east of
Toledo
Waterfowl: Various species of ducks,
geese, Whistling Swans

Wisconsin:

Horicon National Wildlife Refuge
Route 2, Mayville Wisconsin 53050
Location: Eastcentral Wisconsin, drive
east from Waupun on State Route 49 then
south on County Road Z, then follow signs
Waterfowl: Wood Ducks, Mallards, Blue-Winged Teal, Canada Geese

Necedah National Wildlife Refuge
Star Route, Necedah, Wisconsin 54646
Location: Central Wisconsin, off State
Route 21
Waterfowl: Black Ducks, Mallards, Wood
Ducks, Teal, Hooded Mergansers, Canada
Geese

Drake relaxed on water without hen around to show off for

Drake, note bright reddish color on back of crest

Floating drake

Proud drake

Swimming Porchard hen, Wells, England, note position of feet

Porchard drake, Wells, England resembles our Canvasback

Pochard hen, note tail and tertial positions

Black and White Studies and Text

Swans

TRUMPETER SWAN
Cygnus buccinator
62-66 inches

This is the largest of the North American waterfowl and is distinguished from other swans by the narrow salmon colored streak on the edge if its mandibles as well as by its size.

They fly in small V-formations except around their feeding areas where they fly in curved lines or non-regular lines.

They inhabit rivers, lakes and large ponds. They breed in Southeast Alaska and the Canadian Rockies. In winter they can be found in the breeding areas as well as Northwestern Washington. They are an endangered species.

Trumpeter Swan family, the young are called cygnets

Pair, note neck positions

Trumpeter Swan cygnets, note bill detail and necks erect

Trumpeter raising up on surface of water, note neck and wing positions

Swan with cygnets

One month old cygnets, note carriage of necks and heads

Trumpeter walking

Classic threatening position

Threatening Trumpeter, one wing pinioned

Different angle, note bill open

Calmer now, not yet relaxed, note back and wing feathers in moult

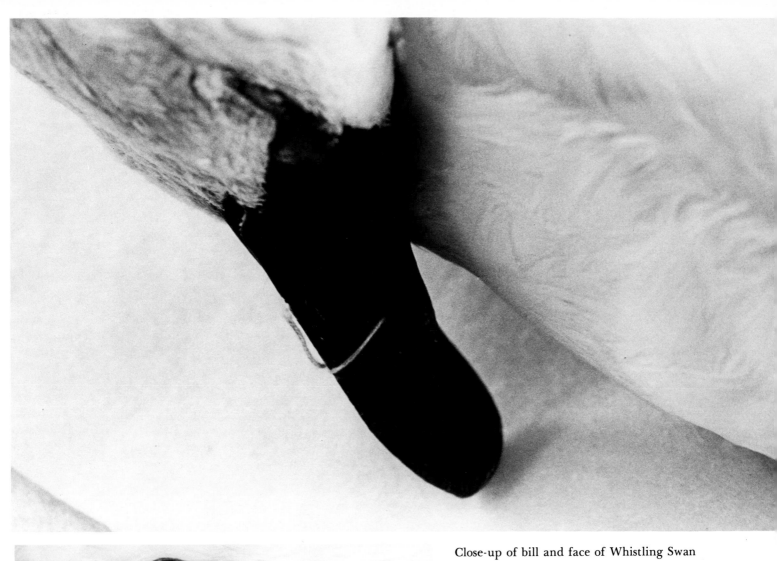

Close-up of bill and face of Whistling Swan

Underneath bill detail

Side and back feather detail, note direction of feathers

Swans

WHISTLING SWAN
Cygnus columbianus
50-54 inches

The neck is held straight, there can be found a yellow mark in front of the eye, however it is not always there.

Their flight is in the V-formation or in non-regular lines, and fast.

This common North American swan inhabits ponds, large rivers, lakes, bays, reservoirs and breeds north of the Arctic Circle from Alaska to the Hudson Bay. In the winter they can be found along the Atlantic coast from the Chesapeake Bay to Currituck Sound and on the Pacific Coast from Southern Alaska to California.

Whistling Swans search the shallow waters for underwater plants and certain mullusks, also feeding on land grasses and some plants, leaves, stems and roots.

Swans

MUTE SWAN
Cygnus olor
57-60 inches

The neck is usually held in an S-curve with the bill inclined downward. The wings can be held raised in an arch above the back. There is a notable large knob at the base of the bill.

The flight pattern of the Mute Swan is usually in the V-formation, or in non-regular lines.

Being a native of Europe, the Mute Swan was introduced to the United States. It inhabits ponds, bays, lakes, large rivers and some wild parts of the East Coast around New York and New Jersey.

Geese

BRANT
Branta bernicla
male: 25 inches
female: 23 inches

   The Brant is a very small goose with a black neck and light sides, slightly larger than a Mallard.
   They are fast flyers, not in the typical V-formation but in loose flocks flying low and irregular.
   They inhabit salt water bays, inlets, marshes, tidal areas and the ocean. Breeding in the Alaskan and Canadian Arctic and in Greenland, they winter along the Atlantic Coast from Massachusetts to North Carolina and along the Pacific Coast from British Columbia down to Baja California.
   They feed on marine algae and eelgrass as well as other grasses, arctic plants and mosses.

Atlantic Brant mount

Brant head, note bill detail

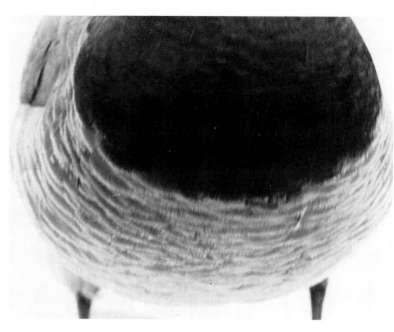

Brant chest and belly, note belly not stark white

Brant side, note feather pattern

Rump area, note long primaries and short tail

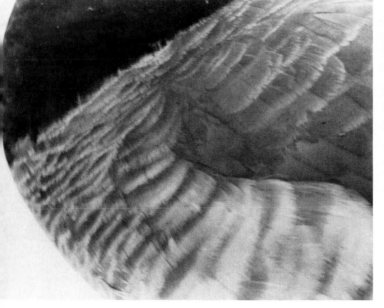

Brant side, note stark division between chest and side feathers

Back detail, note dark secondaries

Brant, different mount

Close-up side feathers for detail

Close-up of secondaries and secondary coverts

Feather pattern for Brant back

Close-up of tail and primaries

Close-up chest, note feather detail

Head detail, front view

Head, note bill detail

Geese

BARNACLE GOOSE
Branta leucopsis
24-27 inches

This medium sized goose is not a native of North America but can be seen from time to time on the eastern coast from Vermont down to North Carolina. It breeds in Greenland and around there and winters in northern Europe. In habit and even in flight the Barnacle Goose resembles the Atlantic Brant. The name it bears is said to be from old myths that they hatched from barnacles.

Barnacle Goose at rest, note feather patterns

Note carriage of tail and relaxed tertial feathers

Pair on water

Standing Blue Goose

Drinking Blue Goose

Underneath Blue Goose, note bill detail

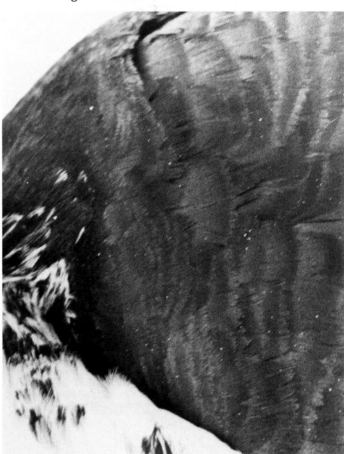

Back detail

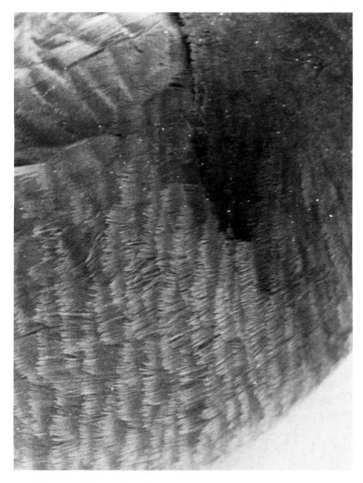

Side and chest detail

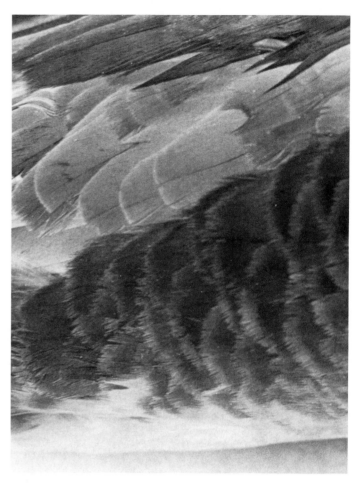

Side feather pattern

Back detail

Tertial area detail

CANADA GOOSE
Branta canadensis
male: 36 inches
female: 35 inches

There are five subspecies of the Canada Goose. These are; 1(Common Canada Goose, 2) Lesser Canada Goose, 3) Richardson's Goose, 4) Western Canada Goose, and 5) Cackling Goose.

The Common Canada Goose is the one referred to mainly as the Canada Goose. The Common and Western Canadas are similar in size and differ only in the shade of their respective plumage, the Western being darker.

Their flight pattern is the typical V-formation, accompanied by much loud honking.

They inhabit aquatic areas, ponds, lakes, marshes, rivers, streams, creeks and bays. They breed in the Arctic southward to California, Montana and Southeast Canada; also in the United States where they are raised in parks, zoos, and refuges. In the winter they can be found throughout the United States.

The Canada Goose feeds on corn fields after the harvest, also grazes in pastures, on grasses and some roots, aquatic plants, grains, occasionally small animals and aquatic life.

Canada Goose, classic suspicious pose

Close-up head, note upper bill detail

Canada Goose preening

Relaxed on pond, note chest nearly disappeared in water and bill detail

Rising up in shallow water to stretch, note curve of neck and shape of chest

Drinking, note shape of neck

Relaxed on water, commonly seen like this

Pair on nest, drake alert, hen still relaxed

Standing Canada, head slightly cocked to look

Hen on nest, note relaxed wings

140

Walking, note foot positions

Classic one-legged resting pose, note angle of leg

EMPEROR GOOSE
Philacte canagica
26-28 inches

The Emperor Geese are similar to the Blue Geese.
Their flight pattern is in a line, fast and low. They inhabit the marine coasts, breeding in Northwestern Alaska and the Arctic Tundra near the sea. They winter on the marine coasts and in the Aleutian Islands.
The Emperors feed mostly on shellfish and seaweeds. On the Tundra they consume berries and various grasses.

Standing Emperor Goose at rest, note feather pattern

Resting Emperor Goose

Standing Emperor Goose

Emperor on water, note carriage of tail

Pair on water, note head, tail and foot positions

Geese

RICHARDSON'S GOOSE
Branta canadensis Hutchinsi
male: 25 inches
female: 23 inches

Next to the Cackling Goose this is the smallest of the geese. Its coloration is like the Common Canada Goose.

It breeds in the eastern Arctic, can be found down along southern Manitoba, Nebraska, Iowa, the Dakotas, and the Mississippi Valley and winters on the Gulf Coast of Mexico.

Standing Richardson's Goose, note tail position and carriage of head

Front view, note feather pattern similar to Canada Goose

Classic relaxed pose

SNOW GOOSE
Anser caerulescens
male: 29 inches
female: 27 inches

The Snow Goose has a white phase in which the entire bird is white with black primaries and a blue phase in which the body is a dark bluish-slaty gray color with white head and neck and coverts under the tail.

They fly in loose formation or disorganized V-formations. Their flight is rapid and often in large flocks.

They inhabit ponds, lakes, marshes, bays and grain fields. The Snow Goose breeds in the Arctic from Alaska to Greenland, wintering along the Atlantic Coast from New Jesey to the Carolinas and along the Gulf Coast; as well as along the Pacific Coast down to Baja California.

The Snows feed much the same as the Canadas but more on native marsh plants and salt marsh plants.

Snow Goose Pair, note black primaries, one wing pinioned on each bird

Feeding pair, note neck shapes, foot positions, feathers
on back of side fallen relaxed

WHITE-FRONTED GOOSE
Anser albifrons
male: 29 inches
female: 27 inches

The name refers to the white band around the face against the bill. Commonly known as the "laughing geese", they are abundant throughout the Northern Hemisphere.

They fly in large flocks in the V-formation or in non-regular lines, with slow wingbeats.

They inhabit ponds, lakes, coastal marine waters, fields, praires and tundra.

Breeding in Alaska and, the Northwestern Canadian Arctic and Greenland; they winter on the Pacific coast, West and Central Gulf Coast, Central Mexico, and usually only in protected areas in the East.

The White-Fronted Goose feeds on nuts, berries, grains, leaves, grasses, and sometimes insects.

White-fronted Goose drinking, note angle of tail

White fronted Goose feeding, note relaxed wing, foot
position

Pair resting after feeding, slightly alert to my approach

Pair feeding on pond edge, note leg and neck positions

Stretching, full extent of one wing, note dark patches on belly, one wing is pinioned

Surface Feeding Ducks

AMERICAN WIGEON (BALDPLATE), (WIDGEON)
Mareca americana
male: 20 inches
female: 18 1/2 inches

The Wigeon is a restless, flightly bird which breeds primarily in North America. (It winters here though some have been seen in the West Indies and South America.)

They fly in non-regular formation, swiftly and in small flocks. They inhabit freshwater ponds, lakes, bays and marshes, also seen in cities and parks throughout the United States.

The Wigeon feeds similarly to the Gadwall on underwater plants, pondweeds, eelgrass and Widgeon grass, often stealing their food from the diving ducks.

American Wigeon drake, note head and tail positions, bill shape

Pair, note hen head shape and small bill

Drake standing, note spread tail

Hen, note bill detail, tail angle

Drake resting, wing gracefully relaxed and spread

Drake head

Drake tertials

Underneath drake head

Drake back

Underneath hen head

Hen tertials, secondary area

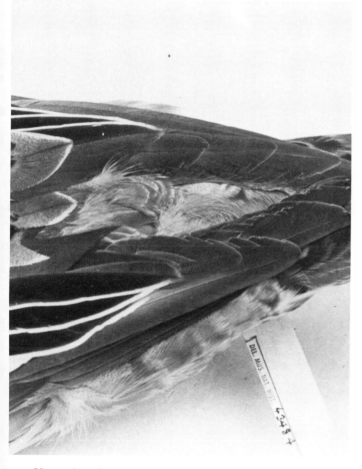

Hen primaries

Underneath hen tail

AMERICAN BLACK DUCK
also; Common Black Duck or Black Duck
Anas rubripes
male: 23 inches
female: 21 1/2 inches

There are two types of Black Duck which are commonly confused. They are the Common, or American Black Duck and the Red-Legged Black Duck or Canadian Black Duck. The latter is the large of the two, however other than that, and the difference in the leg colors, the two are nearly identical. The Common's feet and legs are not usually as red as the Canadians.

The sexes of the two are similar as in the geese, unlike most other ducks.

They fly fast and direct like the Mallard, sometimes in small flocks, V-formations or in lines. They have been known to interbreed with the Mallard.

The Blacks inhabit ponds, lakes, bays, salt water marshes and grain fields. They are widely distributed throughout the Eastern United States.

Standing Black Duck

Rump area, note graceful curve of tertials and small tail

Spread wing tertial feather detail

Rump and tail detail, note center tail feathers shorter and rounded

Tertials, primaries and tail, note placement

Back of head

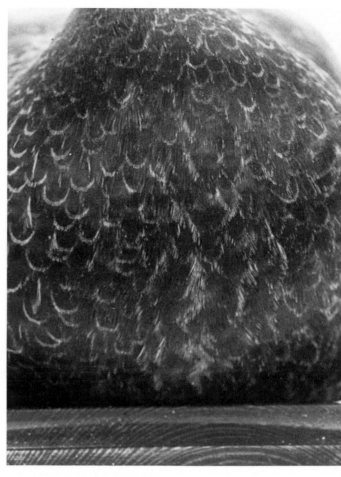

Chest feather detail

Black Duck back

Tertial area

Black Duck head, bill painted, note dark streak through
eye channel

Spread wing secondaries and coverts

Head detail

Underneath belly

Tertial area

Tail and primary area

Upper back

Underneath tail

BLUE-WINGED TEAL
Anas discors
male: 16 inches
female: 15 inches

The Blue-Wing hen is similar to the Green-Winged Teal hen, differing only in shape of their bills; the blue-wings being slightly fatter at the end whereas the Green-Wings tapers at the end, and in the color of their wings; the Blue-Wing having the notable light blue patch on the arm of her wing. The drakes differ more drastically, however they are close in size.

They breed from British Columbia and Southeast Canada south to California, Nevada, Arizona, New Mexico, Texas, Montana, Tennessee, and down the Atlantic to North Carolina.

They feed on grasses, rice, corn, aquatic plants, as well as small insects and aquatic life.

Blue-Winged Teal pair

Standing drake, classic profile

Hen, tail up off water

Pair, note bill shapes, size comparison

Floating pair

Drake, note bill shape and ruffled tertials

Blue-wing Drake

Pair, hen feeding

Floating hen

Hen on pond

Drake standing, note size of head and foot positions

CINNAMON TEAL
Anas cyanoptera
male: 16 inches
female: 15 1/2 inches

This is the only North American duck that is found in the wild only in the western part of the country. They are a very quiet bird, with the hen so closely resembling the Blue-Wing hen that one can rarely tell the difference. They do not, however seem to breed outside their own species.

Their flight patterns are similar to other Teal, however they are easily recognized by the deep cinnamon color of the drake and the soft blue patches on the wings of both sexes.

The Cinnamon Teal inhabit ponds, lakes, streams, sloughs and marshes. They can be found in most of the Western United States and the Southern Canadian Rockies, as well as in some refuges and zoos in the east.

Swimming Cinnamon Teal, note bill shapes

Pair resting, note drakes head back on chest and foot
position in water

Drake, note side feathers starting to moult and foot
position

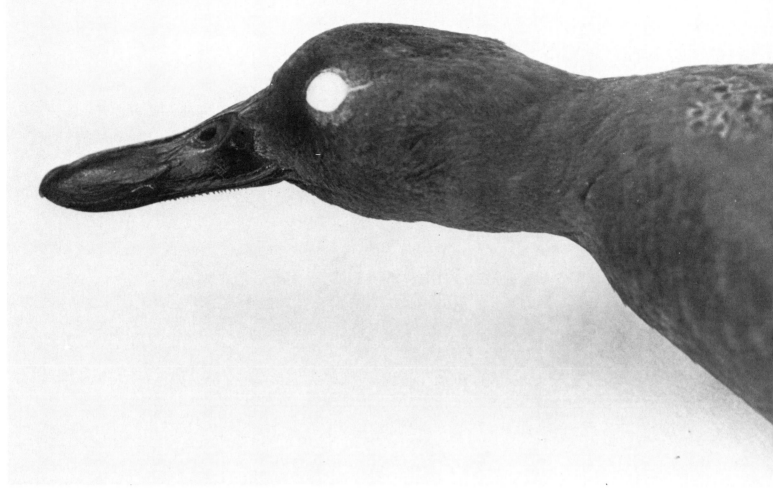

Drake head

Underneath drake head

Drake back feather detail

Tertial area

Drake rump detail

Side of Drake

Hen back and head

Top of hen head

Underneath hen chest

Hen tertials

Surface Feeding Ducks

GADWALL
Anas strepera
male: 21 inches
female: 19 inches

The Gadwall is widely distributed throughout the entire world, yet it is often confused with the Pintail hen and the Pintail immature drake.

They fly fast and direct, with quick wingbeats and in small flocks. They are noticeable in flight from other species as having the only white secondaries of any surface feeders.

The Gadwall inhabits ponds, lakes, rivers and fresh water marshes in Southern Canada and the United States.

The Gadwall is a vegetarian, feeding primarily on underwater plants, pondweeds, eelgrass and widgeon grass.

Gadwell drake on water, note shape of head

Gadwall Drake on water

Hen drinking, note tail position

Pair, both drinking, note tail positions

Drake swimming, head up looking for food

172

Top of hen head

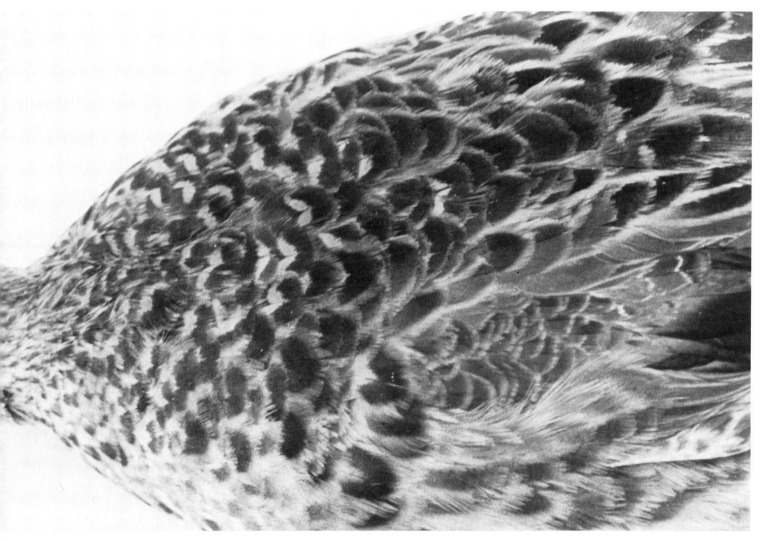

Hen back feather detail

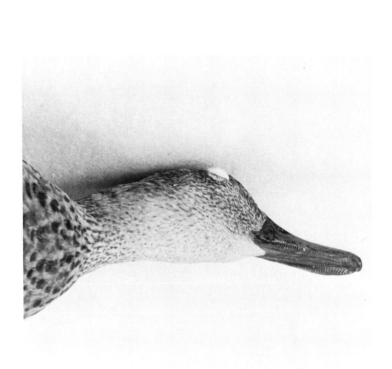

Underneath hen head

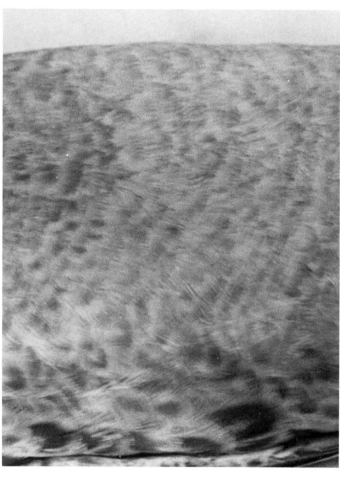

Underneath hen belly

Hen secondaries

Hen primaries

Drake head

Side of drake

Drake back, feather pattern detail

Back of drake

Chest of drake

Underneath drake chest

Drake tertials and primaries

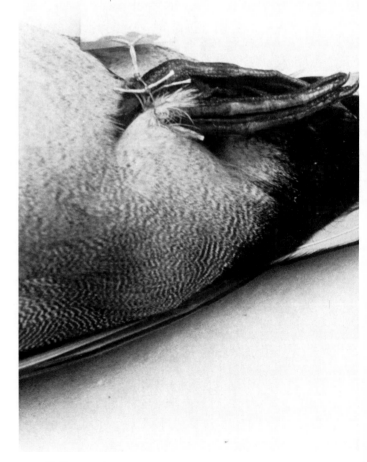

Underneath drake tail

GREEN-WINGED TEAL
Anas crecca
male: 16 inches
female: 14 inches

This duck can be distinguished from its similar European species by the horizontal white line above each wing. They are the smallest of the ducks.

The Green-Wings breed in the Northern United States and Western Canada. They inhabit most of the United States in smooth, shallow ponds, lakes, rivers, streams, marshes and bays.

They feed mostly on the small seeds of water plants, millets, widgeon grass and the like.

Green-Winged Teal Drake standing at rest, note wing position

Hen on water, note tail down

Standing hen, note small bill, leg positions, tail down

Pair on water

Resting drake, note bill detail, feather placement

Drake upper wing extended, note two-tone of secondaries

Drake under wing, hen similar

Underneath primaries of drake wing

Side of drake chest, note pattern of vermiculation changing to dots on chest, very gradual

Hen tail area

Drake, note head position, tertials ruffled in wind

Hen head detail

Standing drake

180

Hen head, note eye channel

Hen primaries, tertial, tail, note tail coverts rounded

Back of hen head

Side of hen chest feather pattern detail

Secondary patch on hen

Hen feather detail

Drake side, note pattern of vermiculations

Drake side, wing up - note under wing and belly

MALLARD
Anas platyrhynchos
male: 23 inches
female: 21 1/2 inches

The Mallard is very likely the most abundant species of waterfowl, inhabiting nearly the entire Northern Hemisphere. It breeds readily with other species.

The Mallards flight is very powerful and direct, flying alone or in loose groups and V-formations.

They inhabit ponds, lakes, rivers, creeks, bays, marshes, and grain fields. Wintering mainly in the Mississippi Valley and in the Gulf States from Texas to Florida, it breeds as far north as Alaska.

All Surface Feeders feed along the surface of the water by scooping up seeds and marsh plants. Rarely diving, they submerge their heads tipping their tails upward. They also eat some small aquatic life as well as seeds, leaves and grasses.

Mallard Drake entering pond, note shape of rump area

Mallard Hen walking, note foot position

Standing hen, note how small her head looks in this position

Resting pair, hens head turned back

185

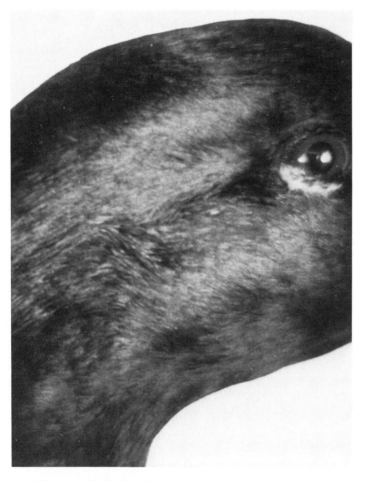

Close-up drake head

Drake tertial and primary detail

Drake neck, note white line edges are feathered, not solid

Underneath rump and tail

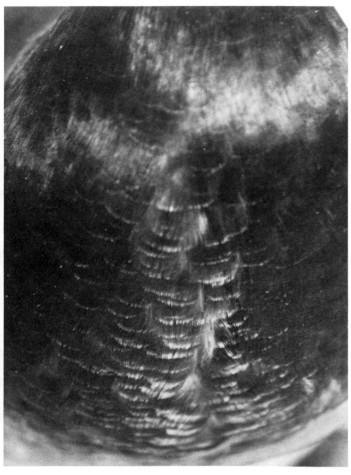

Drake chest, note slight white edges in center towards bottom

Drake wing underneath, hen wing similar

Drake primary detail, open wing

Drake rump and tail detail, note curls

Drake back and shoulders in open wing position

Secondaries and tertials on closed wing of drake, note
upward slope of tertial feather

Underneath drake chest

Drake upper back detail

Drake under belly

Drake tertial and secondary area

Drake primaries

Hen tail area

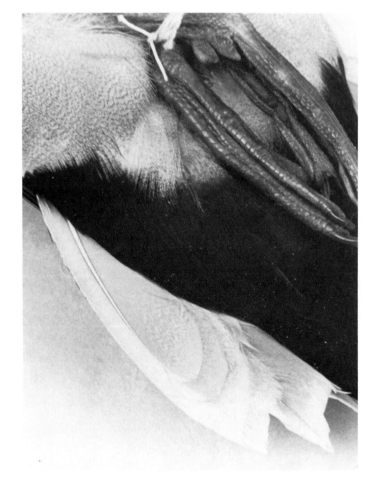

Under drake tail

Underneath hen tail

Hen head, notice feather direction

Hen chest, somewhat darker than the Pintail hen

Hen head, note under bill detail

Underneath hen chest

Hen back, feather detail

Hen tertial area

PINTAIL
Anas acuta
male: 21 inches (with pin)
female: 20 1/2 inches

The long graceful neck and long center tail feather readily distinguish the Pintail drake from other species of waterfowl. The hen can be distinguished from the others by her slender graceful appearance and slightly pointed tail.

Their flight is swift and graceful with a zig-zag descent. When in close to the water the zig-zag diminishes to a glide.

They inhabit freshwater ponds, lakes and marshes, salt water estuaries and bays. They breed and migrate from Alaska to Hawaii and are found all throughout the United States.

The Pintails feed on grains, grasses, weeds, aquatic plants, small aquatic life and insects.

Pintail Hen, note shape of chest with head pulled off to side

Drake, note tail position and graceful curve of neck

Standing drake, note position of primaries, one wing clipped

Drake preening, note indent across chest in this position

Pintail Hen, note thin, long neck and slender tail

Drake, note chest low in water

Back of drake, one wing pinioned

Hen, playful position on water

Hen chest and side, feather pattern detail

Drake, note head position

Drake outstretched wing, note shape of secondaries

Drake rump and tail area, shape of tail coverts differs from other ducks

Drake back and sides, feather pattern detail

Drake head resting on back, bill painted

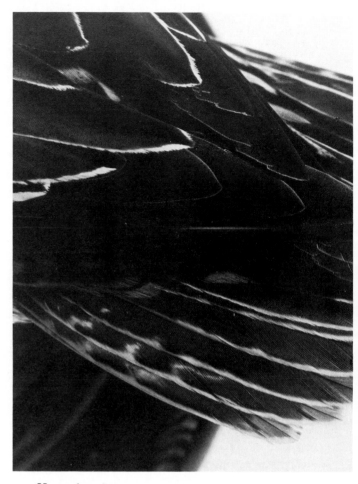

Hen primaries

Hen side and back, feather pattern detail

Standing drake, classic pintail stance

Floating drake, tertials ruffled in wind

Preening hen, note tail off to side

199

SHOVELER
Spatula cylpeata
male: 20 inches
female: 18 1/2 inches

The Shoveler is often referred to as the Spoonbill for its unique bill shape. It is the only North American duck with this type bill. It is the only North American duck with this type bill. It is also commonly found in Europe and Asia.

It breeds in Europe and Asia as well as in North America from Alaska and Canada south to California, New Mexico, Kansas, Nebraska and the Great Lakes region. They winter farther south to Africa, India, China and the West Indies, and are more common in the United States eastward.

They fly in small flocks, direct and slow. Inhabiting ponds, slow moving creeks, freshwater marshes, shallow parts of saltwater bays, and tidal mudflats, the Shoveler feeds on plants, grasses, seeds, small mullusks, and other small aquatic life, as well as small insects, their larvae, and algae.

Shoveler drake, note bill shape and detail

Shoveler hen, note bill shape, leg positions, spread tail

Pair on water, note size difference, tails both slanting upward

Hen, note bill, smallness of head, relaxed wing

Drake, head usually held down close to body, giving appearance of little or no neck

201

Hen, note bill detail

Note bill detail

Hen side, feather detail

Back of hen with side of bill detail

Hen side

Hen primaries

Side of hen chest

Under chest and head detail

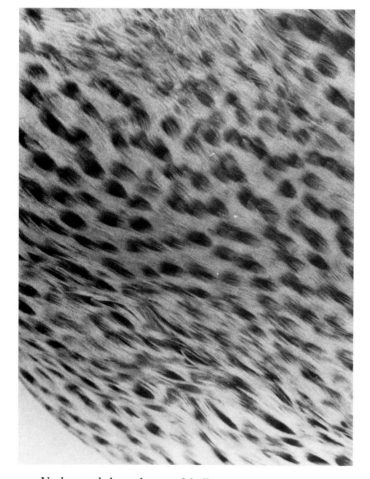

Underneath hen chest and belly

Side of rump, note primaries

WOOD DUCK
Aix sponsa
male: 19 inches
female: 17 inches

The Wood Duck is reputedly the most beautiful of our waterfowl, both the hen and the drake being the most showy of the species. The Woodie is also distinctly North American. Breeding throughout the continent, they winter mainly in the southern states.

Hunted for its tasty flesh as well as its feathers for artificial trout flies, the beautiful Wood Duck very nearly became extinct. Due to the declaration of a closed season on Woodies in 1918, and their being protected until the early 1940's, they have again become abundant.

Their flight is fast and direct, their head held higher than the body.

They inhabit rivers, ponds, marshes and swamps on the edge of forests.

Floating Wood Duck Drakes, classic head positions

Drake swimming, crest relaxed

Drakes, note head and tail positions

Drake, head and tail up, makes classic almost whistling sound when he does this

Drake, relaxed pose

Drake head, bill painted

Hen head, bill painted, note white eye area and light around bill is on face

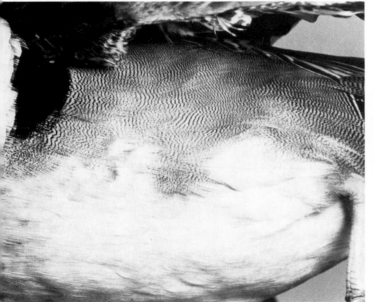

Drake side, note white of belly up onto side

Hen chest and side, note blending of lightness in feather interiors on chest and side

Underneath Drake tail, feather detail

Hen back, note rounded back and tertial feathers

Drake

Swimming drakes, note head positions

Swimming hen, note shape of head and bill

Drakes

Mounted drake

Drake head, bill painted

Side of drake chest

Side of rump and tail area

Diving Ducks

AMERICAN EIDER DUCK
Somateria mollissima
21-27 inches

The American or Common Eider Duck is the largest diving duck. It is of the type of duck that the well known term Eider Down came from. The Eiders have been used also for their skins by the Eskimos.

Their flight is usually slow and heavy and close to the water. They inhabit marine areas almost exclusively and breed on the coasts and islands off the coasts of northern North America from the Aleutians and south to Alaska and from Maine north to Canada and Greenland, Iceland and other areas. It winters on the southern edge of it's breeding range and south to Virginia, Washington, North Carolina and northern Europe. There is sometimes a distinction made between those in North America and those that occur in Europe, one being called the American and the other the Common Eider.

They consume very little plant matter, feeding primarily on mullusks and fish.

American Eider Duck head, note bill detail and slight ridge of feathers on back of cheek and ear area

Resting pair, heads tucked back

Back of drakes head

Bill detail, drake

Drake head, front view, note bill detail

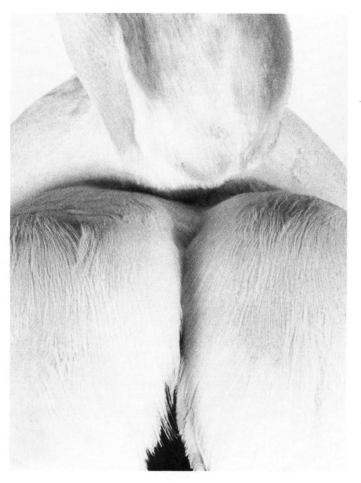

Drake upper back, note streakiness of feathers

Drake tertials and primaries, note how back feathers end at tertials

Drake tail and primaries, note small tail for large bird

Drake underneath, note white patches on sides

American Eider Hen at rest, head back

Hen head, note feathers at front of cheek going into the bill and bill detail

Hen side, note feather pattern

Back of hen head for detail

Hen upper back feather detail

Close-up tertials and primaries

Hen tail and rump feather pattern detail

Underneath hen tail, feather pattern detail

AMERICAN GOLDENEYE
Bucephala clangula
male: 19 inches
female: 17 1/2 inches

This loud, playful duck is sometimes called the whistling duck after the whistling sound their wings make in flight. In courtship the drake is often seen with its head jutting out across the water and also jerking back so that the back of the head rests on the back of the bird, with his bill pointing at the sky. The hen is nearly as peculiar as the drake at this time as she floats on the water completely outstretched with her head jutting forward on the surface of the water.

Their flight is strong and swift, with their wings making the whistling sound. They fly mostly in small flocks, low at first, then circling to gain height.

They inhabit ponds, lakes, rivers, and saltwater areas in winter. They breed in Canada, Alaska and in the Arctic down to eastern Canada and the United States, wintering in the United States and the Atlantic coasts of Canada and southern Alaska, and the Pacific coasts.

Feeding mainly on insects they also consume mullusks, fish and crustaceans.

The Barrow's Goldeneye feeds similarly to the Common Goldeneye, adding somewhat more insects, however.

Their wings make a whistling sound also, though not quite so loud as the Common Goldeneye. The most noticable difference between the two species is the white mark on the faces of the drakes. The Common Goldeneye has a distinctly round white spot whereas the Barrow's Goldeneye has an elongated white mark. The heads of the two are shaped rather differently as well. The Common's being more rounded at the back of the neck, where as the Barrow's is slightly pointed or puffy.

American Goldeneye Hen, note tail position

American Goldeneye Drake, note shape of head at this angle

Drake during classic mating 'dance', head back, bill pointing at the sky

Drake, this position usually follows the previous one

Hen, note shape of head in swimming position

Drake entertaining Red Head pair, note shape of rump
and angle of tail in this stance

Back of drakes head

Drake head, note bill detail

Drake upper back and neck

Drake side, feather pattern detail

Pair, drake starting to dive, hen skimming

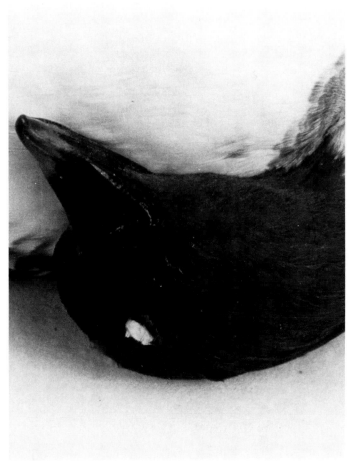

Underneath hen head, note bill detail

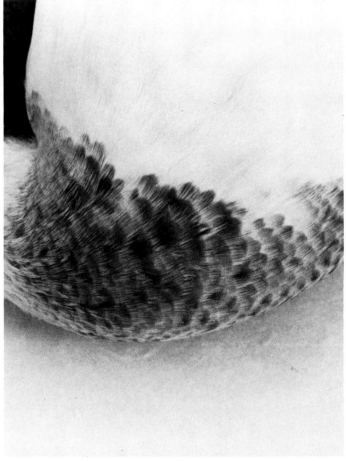

Hen chest

Underneath hen tail

Barrows Goldeneye Drake, note tail position and bill
shape

Drake head, note bill detail

Hen head, note bill detail

Hen side

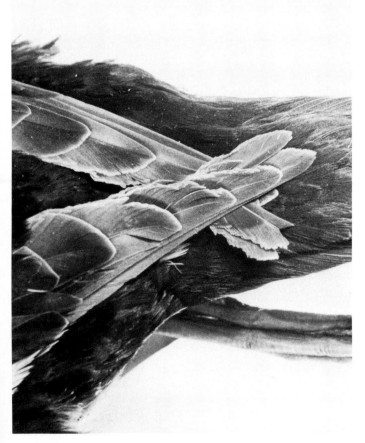

Hen primaries and tail

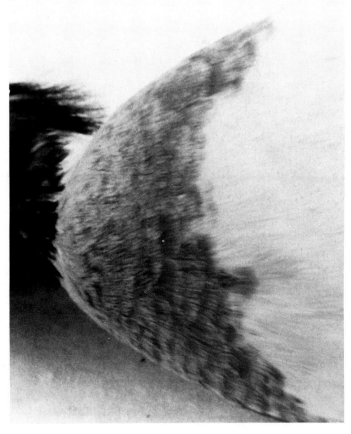

Hen chest

Drake head, another angle

Back of drake

Underneath drake tail

Diving Ducks

Bufflehead
Bucephala albeola
male: 14 1/2 inches
female: 13 1/2 inches

The Buffleheads are also native only in North America and are nearly the smallest of ducks, being only slightly larger than the Teal. They are also tree nesting ducks, like the Goldeneyes they are often linked with.

They fly in small flocks, usually close to the water with fast, powerful wingbeats. They are energetic and playful and are rarely seen still for any length of time.

The little Buffleheads inhabit ponds, rivers, lakes, and marine areas which are protected in the winter. Breeding in parts of Canada and Alaska, they winter in the United States and the Pacific coast of Canada.

They feed on aquatic plants as well as insects, fish and other small aquatic life.

Bufflehead Hen on water, very small, note white patch on face

Drake with head turned back to preen shoulder feathers

Drake side

Hen on water

Drake back and side, primaries long for so small a bird

Drake rump and tail area, note light tail coverts

Hen, very perky position, note tail on water

Sleeping pair on water, note tail positions

Drake on water

Drake head, bill painted

Hen head, note bill detail

Drake head, note bill detail

Drake rump and tail area detail

Drake primary area

Hen mount

Hen head, bill painted

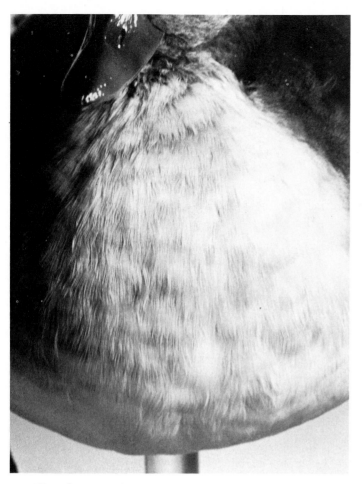

Hen chest, note not pure white

Hen primary area

Hen tail, note small coverts

Underneath hen tail, note coverts

Diving Ducks

CANVASBACKS
Aythya valisineria
male: 22 inches
female: 21 inches

The well known Canvasback is distinctly a species of North America. It is probably the most preferred duck for its flesh, this being commonly attributed to its choice of wild celery as a favorite in its diet. The genus of the wild celery is Vallisneria, which is responsible for the specific name of the Canvasbacks.

Their flight around the feeding grounds is swift, in small close flocks, and in non-regular formation. They migrate in the common V-formation.

They inhabit fresh water ponds, marshes, salt-water marshes and bays, as well as potholes.

Being primarily vegetarians, they feed on aquatic plants, wild celery, seeds and sometimes small aquatic animals.

The Canvasbacks can be found all throughout the United States and western Canada; breeding in Western Canada, Northwestern United States, and wintering along the Atlantic, Pacific and Gulf coasts and inland.

Canvasback Hen, note curve of neck and head slightly inclined downward

Sleeping Canvasback Drake, note head off to side and
bulge of cheek in this position

Same drake, different angle, note tail and primary
position

Sleeping drake

Drake, note tertials

Same Canvasback drake

Sleeping hen, note tail position and head

Preening Hen, unusual elegance for a canvasback

Hen, bill painted, note light area through eye patch

Floating Drake, note bill detail and tail position

Underneath Canvasback drake wing, note separation of
sets of feathers and how curved they are, hen same

Upper wing drake primaries, half spread

Drake upper wing and back, note different vermiculations

Drake head, bill painted

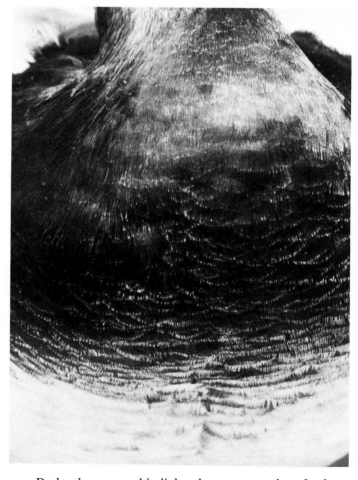

Drake chest, note thin light edge on many chest feathers

Hen looking demure, actually looking in water

Hen side, note size difference in vermiculations on side and back

Hen primaries and tertials, note rounded and pointed tertials

Hen chest, notice it is not solid, light edge to feathers more dominant towards bottom

Diving Ducks

SCAUP
Aythya marila
male: 18 1/2 inches
female: 17 1/2 inches

The Greater Scaup is often referred to as the blue-bill and is commonly mistaken for its slightly smaller relative, the Lesser Scaup. The main differences between the two being; the Greater Scaup has a more greenish irridescence on its head whereas the Lesser Scaup has more purple, the Greater has six or seven primaries with white on them whereas the Lesser has none, the crown of the Lesser stands slightly higher then the Greater, and when in full plumage, the Greaters sides are primarily white with the Lessers having considerably more vermiculations showing.

The Greather Scaups flight is erractic and swift, with a lot of turning, in large, close flocks. They inhabit freshwater ponds, lakes, and rivers in summer.

The Greater Scaups flight is erratic and swift, with a lot of turning, in large, close flocks. They inhabit freshwater ponds, lakes, and rivers in summer. In winter they can be found along the Atlantic, Pacific, and Gulf coasts, in coastal marine waters and the Great Lakes. They breed in Alaska and in northwest Canada.

They feed half on aquatic plants and grasses and half on small aquatic life and insects.

Scaup Hen, usually lighter than the Ring-Necked Hens

Scaup Drake head, bill painted

Hen head, bill painted, not all hens have as much white on face

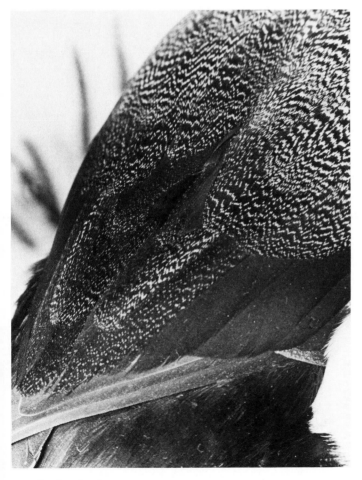

Drake back

Hen side, note secondary patch

Drake rump area, note vermiculations

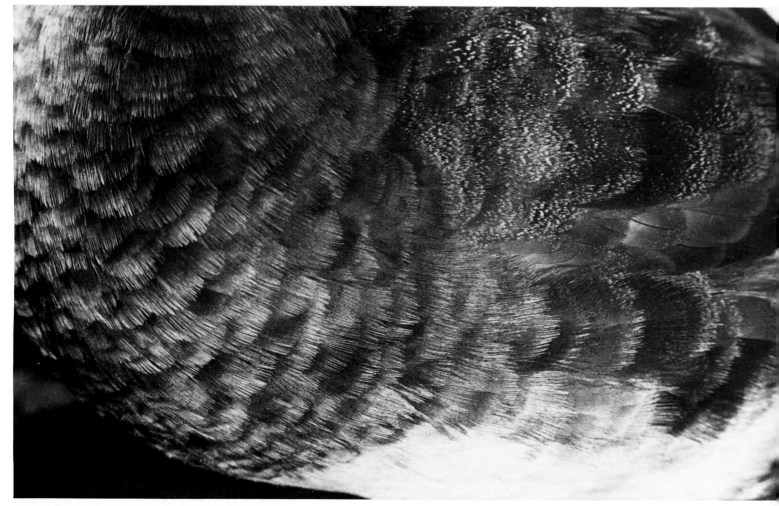

Hen chest, side and back, note vermiculations

Drake, head up to swallow

Hen on water, note tail position

Hen sleeping, note head and tail positions

Hen, note chest low in water

Drake on water

Drake sleeping, note chest position

Hen swimming

Scaup Drake, note tail

Diving Ducks

REDHEAD
Aythya americana
male: 19 3/4 inches
female: 19 inches

Often called the American Pochard for its resemblance and relation to the slightly smaller Common Pochard of Europe, this duck is found all throughout the United States and is quite well known.

It breeds mainly in central Canada and the northcentral United States.

The Redheads fly fast, with quick wingbeats, often in V-formation. They inhabit ponds, bays, lakes and marshes, and winter on the Atlantic and Pacific Coasts as well as in southwestern Canada.

They feed on leaves, stems and aquatic plants, as well as small insects and aquatic life.

The divers have a large lobe on their hind toes, which is not found on the surface feeding ducks, that aids their diving skills.

Red Head Drake resting, note shape of head and chest in this position

242

Drake, note tail on water here

Hen in water, chest and rump fairly even

Drake, note bill detail

Floating pair

Redhead pair with American Goldeneye Drake

Drake, note tail position, head pulled slightly back and roundness of chest

Back of drakes head, note feather pattern

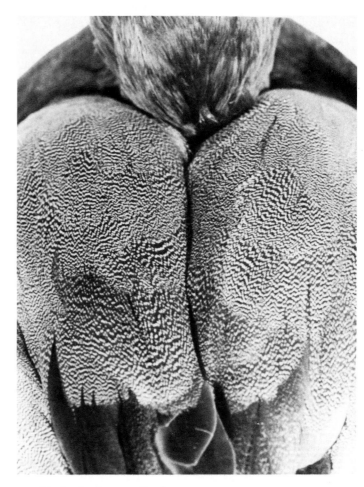

Drake back, note feather patterns

Side of drake, note vermiculations

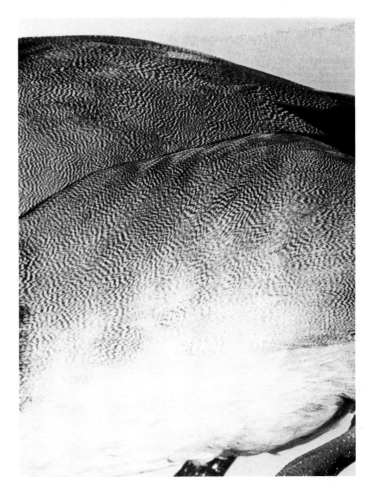

Drake side, note white up onto the side

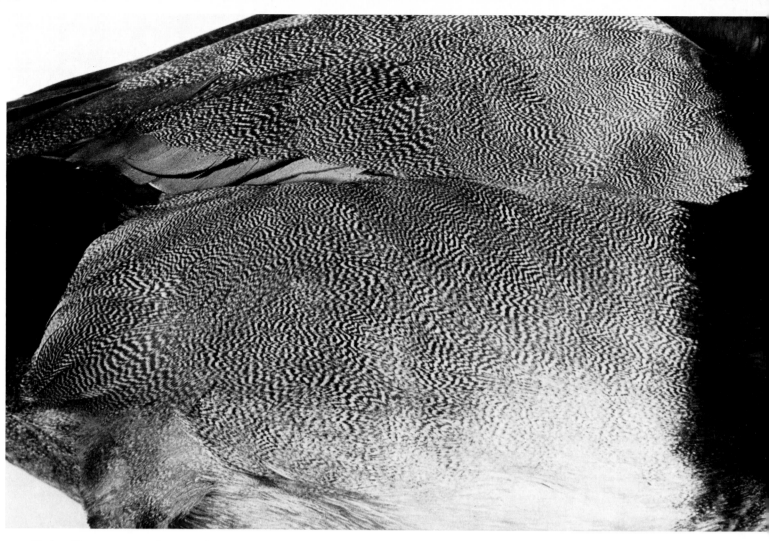

Drake side, note secondary patch

Hen side feather pattern detail

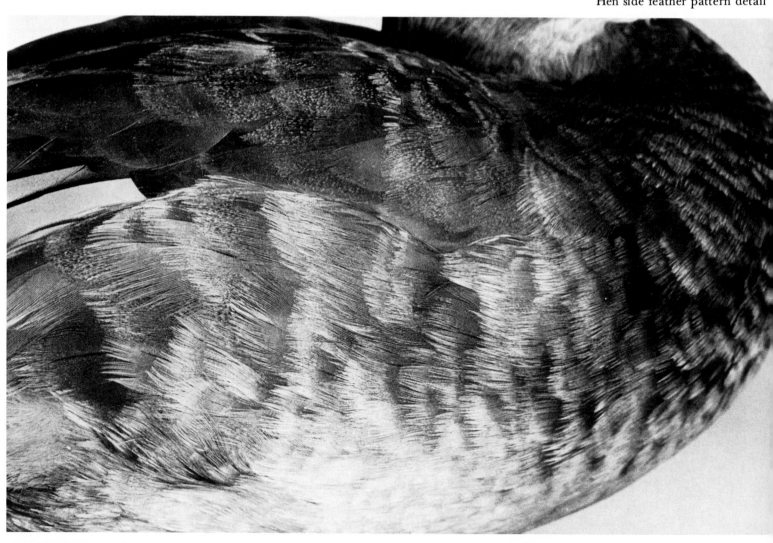

Hen head, note white around eye and lightness towards front of face

Redhead hen feather pattern detail

Overview of drake tail, primaries and rump, note feather patterns

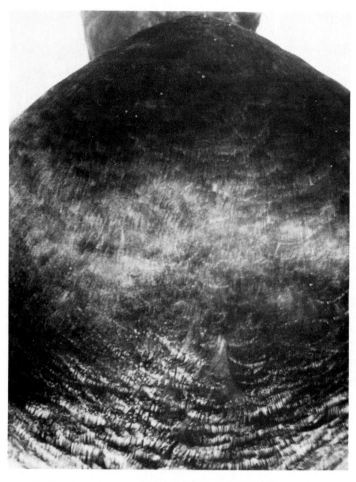

Drake chest, note white edges on some feathers towards bottom

Hen side, note feather pattern and secondary patch

Hen chest, note light edge to all feathers

Hen back, note feather pattern

Hen feather pattern for tertials, primaries, secondaries and rump

Hen tail and primaries for feather pattern

Hen underneath tail and rump, note feather pattern

RING-NECKED DUCK
Aythya collaris
male: 17 inches
female: 16 1/2 inches

These slightly nervous, freshwater ducks are easily confused with the European Tufted Duck. The main difference being in the slight tufts on the crests of both the hen and drake of the Tufted Duck. There is also the fact that the Ring-Necked Ducks have a white ring around their bills and the Tufted Ducks do not.

The Ring-Necked Ducks fly in small flocks, fast and direct. They inhabit ponds, lakes, bays, rivers, marshes, and marine waters where sheltered.

They are a fresh water feeder, consuming aquatic plants, grasses, plant seeds and the larvae and nymphs of insects.

They can be found all through the Canadian Rockies, eastern Canada and south along the Atlantic and Pacific coasts, the Gulf coast and in the southeastern United States.

They breed in Canada, in the western United States and the Northern New England states.

Ring-Necked Drake, note puffiness of head in this position

Hen drinking, note tail position

Drake with head pulled back ready for take off

Hen relaxed, note head pulled off to side and shape of chest in this position

Drake pulling out of water for take off, note shape of neck and head

Drake, head less puffed, note bill detail

Hen, note bill detail and relaxed position on water

Drake, note characteristic 'hook' of white around shoulder

Hen, another angle, note bill detail

Ring-Necked pair, hen drinking

Drake standing out of water to stretch wings

Alert hen, tail on water, chest low in water

Drake, note shape of head straight on

Mergansers

AMERICAN MERGANSER
Mergus merganser
male: 25 1/2 inches
female: 23 1/2 inches

This is the largest of the Mergansers and is not considered good to eat. It is the only North American species of ducks where the hen has a crest and the drake does not.

They inhabit rivers and lakes in forrested areas, while in winter they can be found in lakes, rivers and ponds of open water areas. They breed from Alaska and parts of Canada south to central California, Arizona, New Mexico and also South Dakota, the Great Lakes area and New York, in the North American part of it's breeding range. They also breed throughout parts of Europe, as well as other areas. They winter in the southern parts of their breeding range south.

They feed primarily on fish, consuming also crustaceans, mullusks, insects and some plants.

Beautiful American Merganser Hen mount

Close-up of head, note light under neck and spread crest

Hen side for feather pattern, note direction of feathers

Hen tail and primary area, note distinct pattern of tail coverts and rump feathers

Underneath hen tail and rump detail

Hen side and chest detail

Hen rump area, note shape of secondaries, primaries and tertials

Back of hen head, note crest at this angle

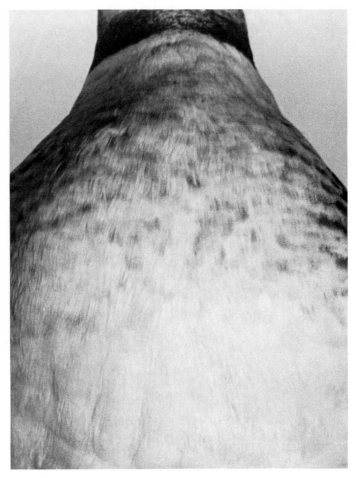

Hen chest for detail

HOODED MERGANSER
Lophodytes cucullatus
male: 18 inches
female: 17 inches

This is the smallest of the Mergansers as well as an exclusive native to North America. They are tree-nesting birds and therefore usually only found in wooded areas.

They inhabit rivers, lakes and ponds in wooded areas, breeding from Alaska and southern Canada south throughout the United States. They winter in British Columbia, the United States central areas, and other parts as well as Mexico and the Gulf Coast and Florida.

Their flight is fast and direct and they feed primarily on fish, amphibians, crustaceans and insects, while including grasses, grains and pondweeds.

Resting Hooded Merganser Hen, note tail flat on water, head way off to side and foot position

Hooded Merganser Drake side, note white of stomach extends up onto side

Drake head detail, bill painted

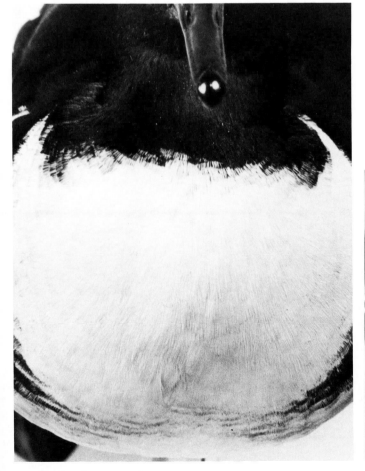

Drake chest area detail

Hen, note tail position, crest half extended

Hen, note how crest is held, chest low in water and shape of bill

Drake, note proportionate size of body to head in this pose

Drake, crest flat, chest low in water, note bill shape

Hen with head up, drinking, note crest in this position, tail flat on water

Drake on water, note crest flattened, tail rests on water

Hen on water, crest fully extended

RED-BREASTED MERGANSER
Mergus serrator
male: 23 inches
female: 21 inches

This merganser is the middle sized one with both the male and female having a crest. They are not favored as game birds but are commonly found throughout North America, Europe and Asia.

They inhabit lakes and rivers and in winter can be found mainly in marine areas. They breed in Alaska and Canada, and in Iceland, Greenland, Ireland and Scotland south, and in North America to Washington as well as other parts of the United States. They winter on the coast from Alaska to California, as well as coastal regions in other parts of the world.

Their diet consists of fish, mullusks, crustaceans and insects.

Red-Breasted Merganser Drake mount

Drake head, note crest feathers

Drake side, note feather patterns and vermiculations

Drake side of chest

Drake rump and tail, note vermiculations into tail coverts and on rump feathers

Hen back and side detail

Back of hen

Hen side

Hen head, note bill detail

Back of drake head

Drake chest

Drake head, note bill detail and flattened crest

Drake upper back

Drake primaries

Drake tail area

Drake underneath

Side of drake

Drake rump area, note vermiculations and odd shape of tail coverts

Drake chest and side feather detail

Drake back feather detail

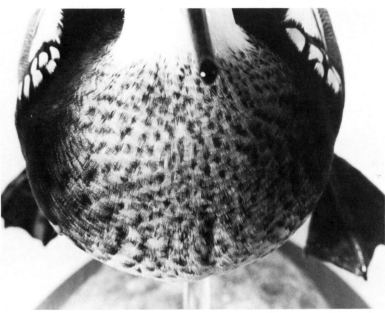
Drake chest and neck

Drake head, bill painted

Drake primaries

Ruddy Duck

Oxyura jamaicensis
male: 14 3/4 inches
female: 14 inches

The curious little Ruddy Duck is another species native only to North America. The drakes brilliant mating plumage, with his little tail sticking up in the air make him easily distinguishable from any other species. His active, noisy mating "dance" is probably the most interesting of all the ducks.

The Ruddies breed from western North America to the Great Lakes area, as well as in Quebec and New England. They winter along the Pacific coast and southern British Columbia down along the Atlantic coast from Massachusetts south and in the southcentral United States.

They run along the surface of the water to take off and seem to have some difficulty. Their flight is noisy and seems somewhat tail-heavy.

The Ruddy feeds on grasses, pondweeds, wild celery, insects and some small shellfish and worms.

Proud looking Ruddy Duck, note rump low in water, chest high

Ruddy Hen resting, not entirely relaxed, note tail
position

Drake more relaxed, note tail position and head pulled
back on chest, also chest and rump more level in water

Preening hen, tail still up

Sleeping hen, note tail

Drake with two hens, note drakes foot placement, and tails and necks of hens

Hen drinking, note tail

Drake

271

Loons

ARTIC LOON
Gavia artica
23-29 inches

This Loon is smaller than the Common Loon and breeds all over the world in tundra areas south, wintering in southern regions of the Mediterranean, Japan, India and northern Mexico.

They inhabit fresh water lakes of tundra regions in summers, wintering on salt water.

They feed mainly in salt water, even when resting at fresh water areas, consuming the same diet as the Common Loon.

Upper back detail

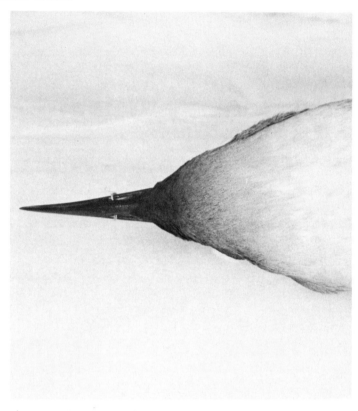

Top of head, Arctic Loon

Side detail

Primary area

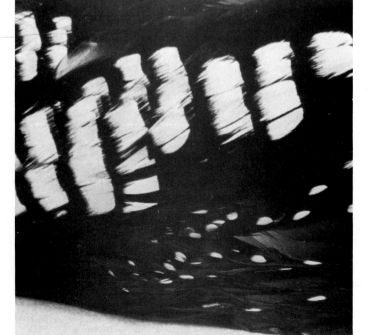

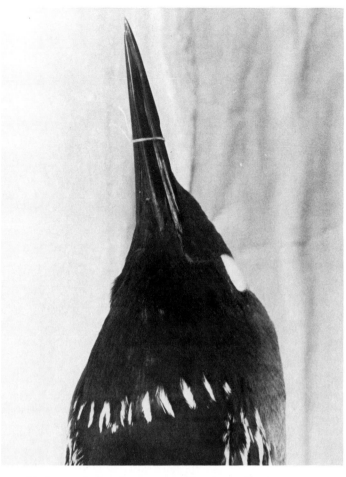

Underneath head, note pattern of streaks

Underneath neck detail

Side detail for feather patterns

Side detail, note white bleeding, into dark feathers

Head, note bill detail

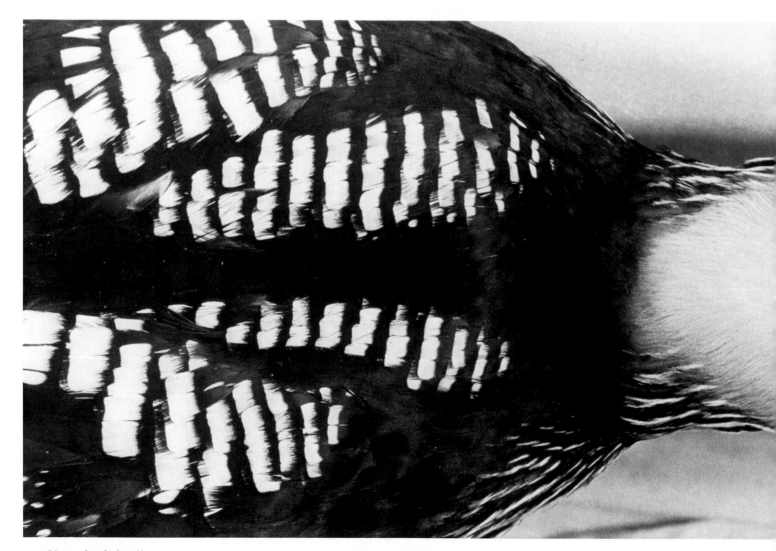

Upper back detail

COMMON LOON
Gavia Immer
28-36 inches

The Loons are native only in the northern part of the northern hemisphere. The sexes are similar and they are primarily aquatic birds. They feed mostly on fish, crestaceans. Also on some aquatic insects and plants, as well as mullusks.

The Common Loon breeds from Greenland, Iceland and Alaska south to New England, Michigan, North Dakota and Northern California. They winter from Maine and the Great Lakes and southern Alaska south, primarily along both coasts. They nest in fresh water areas, yet in winter can be found mainly on salt water.

They are excellent swimmers but rise from the water with trouble, once airborne their flight is swift.

Head and bill detail, Common Loon

Back detail

Side of back for feather patterns

Underneath head detail, note white pattern

Side detail

Primaries and rump area

276

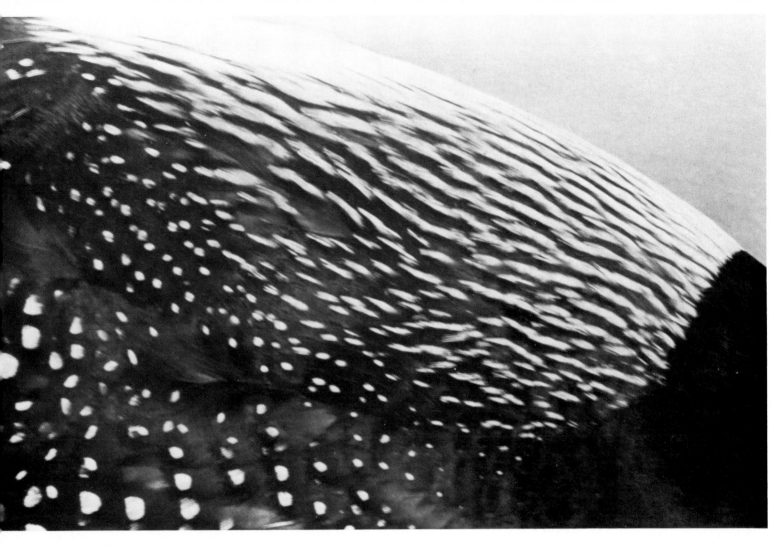

Side of chest detail, note white pattern

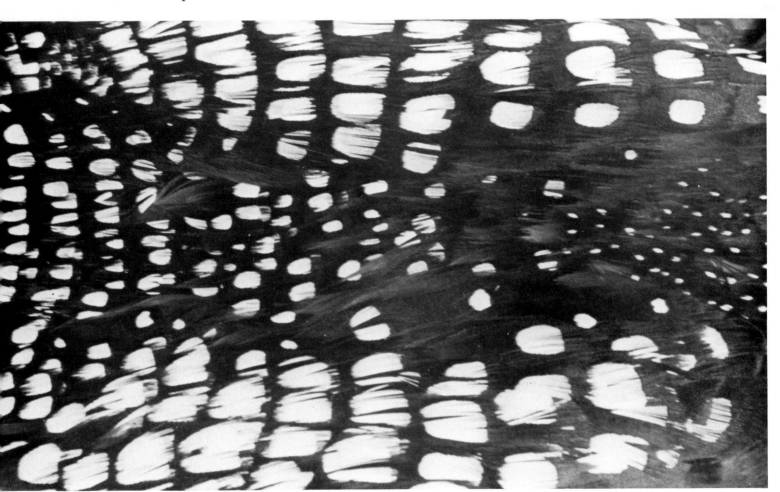

Back detail for feather pattern

RUBY-THROATED LOON
Gavia Stellata
24-27 inches

This is the smallest of the Loons, which results in easier take - off than the other, larger Loons.

They breed in tundra areas in all parts of the world, from Iceland to Greenland and other areas. They winter from their southern breeding areas to the Mediterranean, Japan, northern Mexico and northern Florida.

They feed much the same as the Common Loon except for plants.

Top of head and bill detail

Underneath head detail

Head and bill detail, Ruby-Throated Loon

Side of chest and neck for detail

Primary area

Side of bird

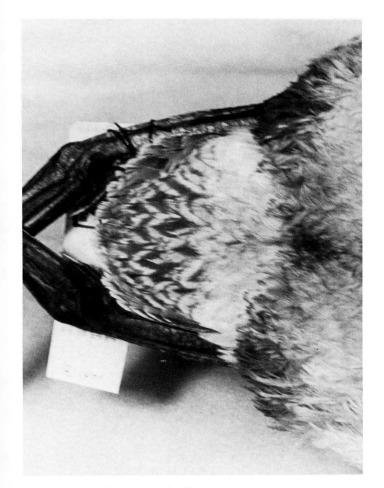

Underneath rump and tail

Back of bird

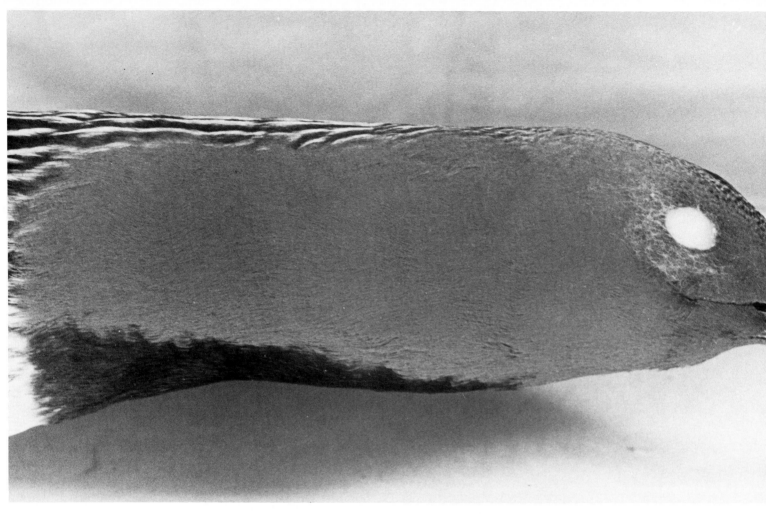

Side of head detail

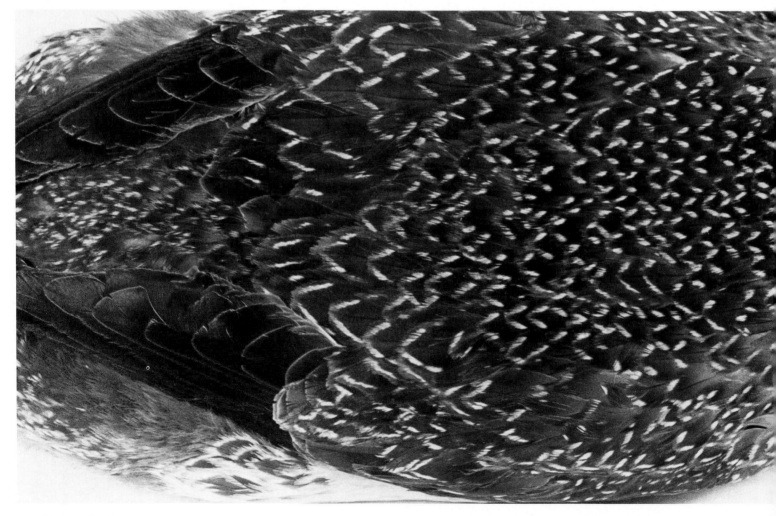

Back and primary area

YELLOW-BILLED LOON
Gavia Adamsii
30-36 inches

This Loon is very much like the Common Loon in appearance, except for the color and shape of it's bill. The Yellow-Billed Loon is also somewhat larger than the Common; being the largest of the loons.

They inhabit fresh water rivers and lakes in northern tundra areas in summer, wintering on coastal waters.

Most other charachterists of the Yellow-Billed Loon closely resembles those of the Common Loon.

Yellow-Billed Loon head, note bill detail

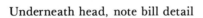

Underneath head, note bill detail

Back, note feather pattern

Primary detail

Grebes

The Grebes are small water birds, fast swimmers, excellant divers and not very adept on land. They require large areas of water for take - off and landing and their flight is not one of their best features.

They feed mainly on fish and other aquatic animals as well as some aquatic plants.

EARED GREBE
Podiceps caspicus
12 1/2-13 1/2 inches

The Eared Grebe resembles the Horned Grebe and is usually smaller. They breed and winter in America, Africa, Europe and Asia. In north America they breed from British Columbia, Canada south to California, central Arizona and parts of New Mexico and Texas. They winter in marine waters or the Pacific and inland from California, Nevada, Mexico and Texas.

Often seen in large flocks during migration and in the winter, they breed mainly in bays and coves of fresh water lakes and ponds.

They feed primarily on aquatic insects and animals, also some fish.

HORNED GREBE
Podiceps curitus
12 1/2-15 inches

Usually much smaller than the Red-Necked Grebe, the Horned Grebe is recongnizable at a distance by the prominance of it's crest, or "horns".

It nests in parts of Alaska south to northwest Washington, central Idaho and parts of Montana, North Dakota and Minnesota. The Horned Grebe winters on the coasts to southern California and into Texas migrating inland, also found in Europe and Asia.

During the breeding season they inhabit open water ponds and marshes and lakes and rivers, wintering on inland waters, and marine waters, usually not very far off shore.

They feed primarily on small aquatic life.

PIED-BILLED GREBE
Podilymbus podiceps
12-15 inches

This small Grebe has a much smaller bill than any of the other Grebes and is found in wider range than any of the other Grebes.

They breed throughout parts of Canada south to Chile and Argentina, wintering south around the Gulf Coast, Texas, Mexico and southeastern United States, south to Argentina.

They feed on small fish, crayfish and insects.

RED-NECKED GREBE
Podiceps grisegena
17-22 inches

The Red-Necked Grebe is not a pleasant bird to listen to, especially during breeding season. They breed from Alaska, Central Yukon, parts of Ontario to northeast Washington, northern Idaho mountains and North Dakota and parts of Minnesota. They winter on the coasts down to southern California and on the eastern coast down to Florida.

In summer they inhabit inland waters, wintering mainly in marine waters.

WESTERN GREBE
Aechmophorus occidentalis
22-29 inches

The Western Grebe, as indicated by its name, is common in the East Western United States. It breeds in freshwaters from Canada to California, northern Arizona and parts of Colorado, Nebraska and South Dakota.

They winter along the Pacific Coast from Alaska south to Mexico, also found inland in California, Nevada and Washington.

They inhabit fresh and salt water areas, also found in sheltered marine areas. Feeding mostly on small fish, they also eat insects, mullusks, and other small marine life.

American Coot
Fulica americana
13-16 inches

Coots are great swimmers and great divers, the American Coot being the only North American species of Coot. From a distance the Coot looks like small headed ducks on the water. They are most comical when "skipping" or running along the water when chased or frightened.

They breed from parts of Canada to Wisconsin and Michigan south to California, Nicaragua, Panama and the Gulf Coast, Florida, and Jamaica, and Hawaii through the West Indies. They winter in the south around Arizona, Texas, Mexico and in Maryland, south to Panama and to the Bahamas.

The Coot inhabit fresh water ponds, lakes, and marshes, field, meadows and salt water areas in winter.

They feed on vegetables, fish and other small aquatic life. They are usually found in large flocks, and often prefer wild celery and other grasses which are also preferred by many ducks.

Side feathers detail

Underneath neck detail

Side of neck and chest, note pattern of streaks

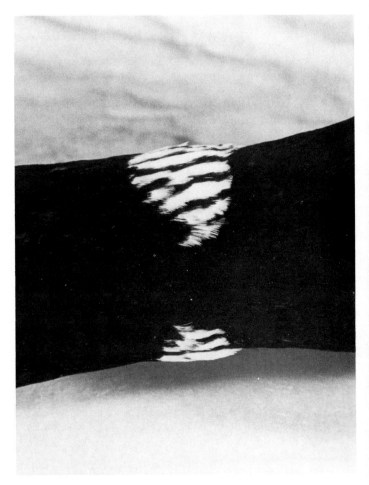

Side of rump detail

Neck and upper back area

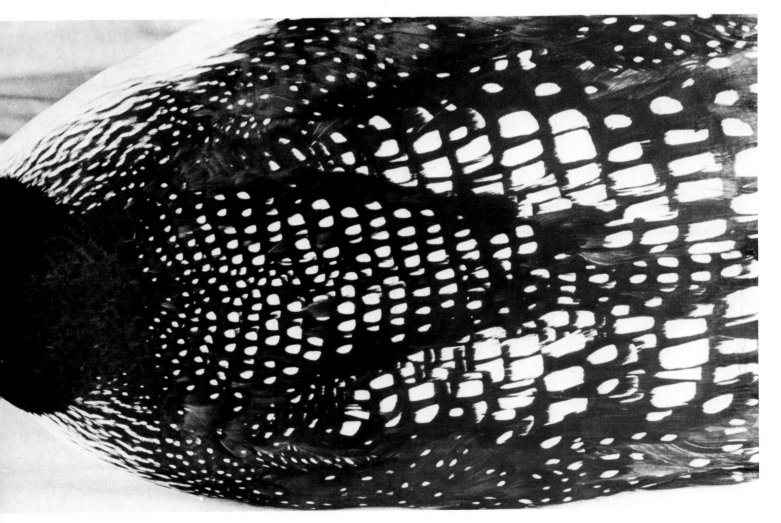

Back, for detail of feathers

Other Species

FULVOUS WHISTLING DUCK (FULVOUS TREE DUCK)
Dendrocygna bicolor
18-21 inches

These unusually long-legged ducks rather remind one of the geese by their long necks and gooselike habits. The word Fulvous refers to the yellowish brown or tawny color of most of the bird. These ducks are seldom actually found in trees, preferring to nest in grasses on the ground, they are occasionally forced to nest in the hollows of trees.

Their flight is strong with somewhat slower wingbeats than most other ducks. They inhabit marshes that are of fresh water and cultivated areas in the tropics and subtropics. They can be found feeding in cornfields and also eat grass seeds and weeds.

Fulvous Whistling Duck standing, note exceptionally long legs

On water, rather like the Teal in size

Pair on water, note slight point on drakes head

Note how far back the legs are on the body

Swimming, note how much of under body is in the water

Pair, note large feet and carriage of chests is high

Standing Fulvous Whistling Duck, chest high

Other Species

MANDARIN DUCK
Aix galericulata

This spectacular species is not native to North America and can not be found here in the wild. They can, however, be found throughout the United States in captivity. They are probably the showiest species, with the Wood Ducks running a close second. Like their relative, the Wood Duck, their feathers are more popular than their flesh. They are native Asian birds and have been successfully introduced to other areas such as Great Britain. The Mandarin hen is very similar to the Woodie hen.

Mandarin Drake, note tail downward, head pulled back
on chest, chest puffed up

Floating idle, note tail position

Sitting idle on water, note position of crest

Mandarin front detail, note bill shape

Drake with a Mallard Hen mate

Photography Hints

When photographing waterfowl in their habitats, there are a few simple rules to follow. If you use these guidelines, you should be able to get well exposed, clear pictures.

Keep in mind that you are photographing an object which *rarely* stands completely still. What this means is that your subject will invariably reduce your chances of absolute clarity because of it's movement. With the guidelines, however, you should be able to reduce the blur this produces on film to a minimum.

A. **Use fast film**

1. Unless you are shooting in total sunlight, a very high film speed is recommended.

2. Kodak now produces two very fine films for this purpose; ASA 400 and ASA 1000. Most of the outdoor color in this book was done with Kodak's ASA 400 film.

B. **Use a Tripod**

1. Whenever and wherever possible you should have your camera on a tripod to reduce camera shake.

C. **Use fast shutter speeds**

1. The faster shutter speed you use, the shorter amount of time your subject has to move.

2. If the shutter speed is 250 or faster, your subject should "freeze" no matter how fast it is moving.

3. 125 is fast enough, especially if you can not have the f-stop at f6 or f8 or closed down further (larger numbers) at 250.

D. **Use f8 - f16**

1. The maximum clarity of any lens is in the center, this means if your aperture (or f-number) is opened all the way (or on smaller than f-6), then you are not getting maximum clarity. This means your subject could still appear slightly blurred even though you focused perfectly. This is more pronounced when using longer lenses. This tip aided me more than any other.

E. **The ideal situation**

1. ASA 400 or 1000 by Kodak, or other ASA in total sunlight.

2. Shutter speed 250 or faster (500-1000)

3. f-8 to f-16

4. Camera on a tripod

5. Also remember to pay attention to what you want framed in the picture and watch your backgrounds!

Bibliography

Heintzelman, Donald S. *North American Ducks, Geese and Swans.* New York: Winchester Press, 1978.

Kitching, Jessie. *Birdwatchers Guide to Wildlife Sanctuaries.* New York: Arco Publishing Company, Inc., 1975, 1976.

Kortright, F.H. *The Ducks, Geese and Swans of North America.* Washington, D.C.: The Stackpole Company and Wildlife Management Institute. Copyright 1942, 1953, 1967 Wildlife Management Institute.

Meanley, Brooke. *Waterfowl of the Chesapeake Bay Country.* Tidewater Publishers, 1982.

National Wildlife Federation. *1983 Conservation Directory.* Washington, D.C.: copyright 1983.

Reilly, Edgar M., Junior. *The Audobon Illustrated Handbook of American Birds.* McGraw-Hill, Inc. Sponsored by The National Audobon Society. Copyright 1968.

Riley, William and Laura. *Guide to the National Wildlife Refuges.* Garden City: Anchor Press/Doubleday, 1979.

United States Department of the Interior. *Waterfowl Tomorrow.* Washington: United States Government Printing Office, 1964.

Veasey, William with Hull, Cary Schuler. *Waterfowl Carving: Blue Ribbon Techniques.* Exton: Schiffer Publishing Limited, 1982.

Index